CHICKEN SOUP FOR THE TEENAGE SOUL ON LOVE & FRIENDSHIP

CHICKEN SOUP FOR THE TEENAGE SOUL ON LOVE & FRIENDSHIP

Jack Canfield
Mark Victor Hansen
Kimberly Kirberger

SCHOLASTIC INC.
New York   Toronto   London   Auckland   Sydney
Mexico City   New Delhi   Hong Kong   Buenos Aires

We would like to acknowledge the following publishers and individuals for permission to reprint the following material. (Note: The stories that were penned anonymously, that are public domain, or that were written by Jack Canfield, Mark Victor Hansen or Kimberly Kirberger are not included in this listing.)

The Boy at Band Camp. Reprinted by permission of Molly Gaebler. ©2001 Molly Gaebler.

Fugue. Reprinted by permission of Don Keys. ©2002 Don Keys.

Just One Look, That's All It Took. Reprinted by permission of Dan Mulhausen. ©2000 Dan Mulhausen.

Friends for Life. Reprinted by permission of Tina Leeds. ©2000 Tina Leeds.

Impossible Things Can Happen. Reprinted by permission of Pegah Vaghaye. ©2000 Pegah Vaghaye.

You Are All of This to Me. Reprinted by permission of Melissa Collette. ©2001 Melissa Collette.

(Continued on page 297)

ISBN 0-439-57637-7

With love we dedicate this book to
Mitch Claspy and Tasha Boucher
for all the work you do for teens.

Contents

4. TOUGH TIMES

5. FAMILY AND LOVE

6. ACTS OF KINDNESS

7. GROWING UP

Acknowledgments

Chicken Soup for the Teenage Soul on Love & Friendship was a joy to work on. As is always the case, writing and compiling this book required the hard work and dedication of many people. The following people were invaluable throughout the process.

Mitch Claspy and Tasha Boucher—for giving so much to this project that it can't be expressed in words. Your names should really be on the cover of this book. As well as being hard workers, you are also two of Kim's most treasured friends.

Our families are a huge part of our inspiration and the force that drives us to give what we can of ourselves to make the world a better place:

Jesse Kirberger, Kim's son—you mean the world to Kim and are the inspiration for all she does.

Inga, Travis, Riley, Christopher, Oran and Kyle—for the love and support you bring to Jack's world.

Patty, Elisabeth and Melanie Hansen—for lovingly being there for Mark.

Kim and Jack's mother, Ellen Taylor—for supporting them no matter what.

Fred Angelis, Kim and Jack's father—for all your love and kindness.

Mark's parents, Paul and Una—for being a never-ending source of support.

In addition to their hard work and support, our staff teaches us the meaning of "love and friendship" as well. They are:

Lisa Wood-Vazquez—for always brightening our day with your incredibly positive attitude and for keeping Kim's office and life running smoothly.

Patty Aubery—for running the entire show so gracefully. We couldn't do any of this without you.

Heather McNamara and D'ette Corona—for producing the final manuscript with magnificent ease, finesse and care. We love working with you two.

Our teen staff members continually teach and enlighten us. We feel fortunate to have such beautiful young souls around us on a daily basis. They are selfless in their support, and we couldn't do it without them. Our deepest thank-yous to:

Christine Kalinowski—for your sweetness and for being more mature than most adults.

Brie Gorlitsky—for caring so much about your fellow teens.

Hayley Gibson—for being such a hard worker and contributing so much.

Jenny Sharaf—for your excellent reading and writing skills.

The following teenagers took precious time out of their lives to read the original manuscript, help us make the final selections and make invaluable comments on how to improve the book. A huge thank-you to:

Brian Chan, Kelvin Chan, Brenna Cibley, Elisabeth Day, Corey Dweck, Bethany Emes, Lauri Engman, Theresa Galeani, Hayley Gibson, Brie Gorlitsky, Britney Graham, Sara Guilliam, Christine Kalinowski, Courtney King,

Miranda Lee, Erica Leonberg, Sarah McCulloch, Katrina Mumaw, Megan Perez, Nicole Peterson, Pamela Peterson, Jamie Rolland, Helen Scammell, Lisa Schofield, Samuel Schultz, Jenny Sharaf, Blaire Tacquard, Jessica Woodruff, and Lindsay Yourist.

Leslie Riskin—for your vivacity and tenacity. You work incredibly hard to secure our permissions, and you are such a joy to work with in the process.

Nancy Mitchell-Autio, LeAnn Thieman, Veronica Romero, Robin Yerian, Teresa Esparza, Vince Wong, Cindy Holland, Stephanie Thatcher, Kathy Brennan-Thompson, Dana Drobny, Michelle Adams, Dave Coleman, Laurie Hartman, Irene Dunlap, Jody Emme, Maria Nickless, Dee Dee Romanello, Gina Romanello, Brittany Shaw, Shanna Vieyra and Lisa Williams, for your commitment, dedication, professionalism and making sure Jack's and Mark's offices run so smoothly.

Our publicist, Sharon House, has been passionate about the teen books since she was brought onto our team. We are very grateful to you, Sharon.

We want to thank the staff of our wonderful publisher, Health Communications:

Peter Vegso, our publisher, for your wisdom and support. Thanks for continuing to publish books that make a difference for teens.

Lisa Drucker and Susan Tobias, our amazingly talented editors at Health Communications, who are such a joy to work with. We adore you both.

Kim Weiss, for her talented PR work and for being a great friend.

Paola Fernandez, who completes Health Communications' awesome publicity team, and whose hard work continues to keep these books on the bestseller lists.

Terry Burke and Kelly Maragni, without whose sales

and marketing skills the success of the *Chicken Soup* books would not be what it is today.

Randee Feldman, for your spirited coordination and support of all the *Chicken Soup* projects.

Thanks to the art department at Health Communications, for your talent, creativity and enduring patience in producing designs that capture the essence of *Chicken Soup*: Larissa Hise Henoch, Lawna Patterson Oldfield, Andrea Perrine Brower, Lisa Camp, Anthony Clausi and Dawn Grove.

Teri Peluso, Christine Belleris, Patricia McConnell, Karen Ornstein and the rest of the Health Communications staff—you give so much of yourselves in order to make these books a success.

Introduction

Dear Teens,

Since the first *Chicken Soup for the Teenage Soul* book was released in 1997, we have been receiving hundreds of letters a day from teens like you—and possibly even you! We receive so many letters about love and friendship that we felt it was time to compile a book dedicated entirely to these two important subjects.

Love and friendship are top priorities for nearly everyone, but especially for teenagers. Your friends are almost as important as your family, and the lessons you learn from friends, boyfriends and girlfriends are lessons that shape who you are and who you will become as an adult.

The stories in this book are about relationships and the lessons we learn from them. It is our hope that you will see yourself in many of these stories, and that you will realize that you are not alone in the trials that come with any friendship or relationship. May you discover from these stories, and in your own life, how amazing friendships can be and how blessed we all are when love is a part of our lives.

We hope you enjoy reading this book and that you find comfort and guidance within these pages.

All our love,
Kimberly, Jack and Mark

Share with Us

Most of the stories in this book were written by teens like you. We would like to invite you to send us stories you would like to see published in future editions of *Chicken Soup for the Teenage Soul.*

We would also love to hear your reactions to the stories in this book. Please let us know what your favorite stories are and how they affected you.

Please send submissions to:

Chicken Soup for the Teenage Soul
P.O. Box 936
Pacific Palisades, CA 90272
fax: 310-573-3657
e-mail for stories: *stories@iam4teens.com*
e-mail for letters: *letters@iam4teens.com*

Come visit our Web site:
www.iam4teens.com

You can also visit the *Chicken Soup for the Soul* site at:
www.chickensoup.com

We hope you enjoy reading this book as much as we enjoyed compiling, editing and writing it.

1

FALLING IN LOVE

Love doesn't make the world go around.
Love is what makes the ride worthwhile.

Franklin P. Jones

The Boy at Band Camp

Within your heart, keep one still, secret spot where dreams may go.

Louise Driscoll

Strains of Mariah Carey floated in the background as we held each other close and swayed to the rhythm of the music. I hadn't expected us to be so intimate when I asked the guy who had been my best friend at summer camp to dance. But as my head rested on his shoulder and his arms wrapped around my torso, I realized that I had fallen head-over-heels for this guy. My timing had never been worse. It was the farewell dance at summer camp, the night before we left, and I was just realizing that I wanted to be with him. Furthermore, I had gone to middle school with him for the past two years, and I had never thought twice about the fact that I saw him literally six times a day. Then, he was just the annoying little boy who threw goldfish at my friends and me during lunch. But now he was the boy who would save me a seat at breakfast and write messages on my hand. The one with the cute smile and jokes that would make me giddy with laughter. And now I was dancing with him, the wonder boy. I had never been more content in my entire life. The song's last notes faded out and we just stood, locked in our embrace. Neither of us wanted to move; the moment was too perfect. However, we were soon interrupted by the loud drumbeat of a Blink-182 song. We jumped apart, startled.

"Whoa," he said, shyly smiling. "That scared me." I smiled back at him and nodded in agreement. We were soon joined by a group of our friends and began jumping around to the muffled words of "All the Small Things."

It was now 9:30 P.M., time for us to crawl into our sleeping bags and whisper under the pillows. I was walking back to my cabin, grinning from ear to ear in the dark. Unexpectedly, someone jumped onto my back, causing me to stumble. I looked up to see who had attacked me and it turned out to be my friends Beth and Kari.

"So . . . Molly!" Beth said to me, with a smirk on her face.

"Y . . . yes?" I stammered, turning red.

"You and Brian, eh?" teased Kari.

All I could do was smile and laugh, but that was enough to send my friends into squealing fits of, "Oh my GOD!" and, "I knew it!" Satisfied that they had pulled the latest gossip out of me, they pranced off to tell the rest of my cabin. I didn't really care. They were all my best friends, and they would have found out sooner or later.

The next morning was concert day. We all had rehearsal in between packing our suitcases. I walked to the piano room for my ten o'clock run-through. I rushed through my piece and didn't bother to stick around for my feedback. Instead, I left the amphitheater where the orchestra was rehearsing and joined a group of my friends who were exchanging phone numbers and e-mail addresses.

"Molly! You're here!" said one of them.

"Yeah, I tried to get out of rehearsal as soon as possible,"

I replied as I grabbed a handful of pretzels from a bowl on the bench.

We started talking about nothing in particular, laughing and joking about anything and everything. Suddenly, Elise shouted "Hey Molly! Look who it is!" and pointed to my right. Snapping my head around, I saw Brian strolling up the hill to the amphitheater. I blushed and waved and quickly turned back to the conversation. He joined us and I could feel the rickety bench we were sitting on sink lower with his weight. Everyone's eyes were on me. I fidgeted with my bracelets while the silence grew.

"What's going on?" he asked, with a sincerely confused look on his face. Out of fear that one of my friends would embarrass me in front of him, I jumped up, mumbled something about forgetting to pack my sweatshirt and ran off in the direction of my cabin. Even though nothing extremely unordinary had happened, I couldn't help feeling embarrassed. I walked down to the beach instead of to my cabin and sat down on the sand. I felt like being alone for a while.

I wiped my tears on my sleeve while hugging all my friends. I couldn't believe it was time to go home already! Our time together had gone by so fast. I would have to wait a whole year before I would see these people again, I reminded myself as I heaved my overflowing duffel bag into the trunk of the car. All around me, cameras flashed, pens were scribbling digits, and people sobbed into each other's shoulders. Saying good-bye is always hard. But I was ready to go. I had seen everyone I needed to, until I heard my name being yelled from across the way.

"Molly!"

I turned around to see who had called my name. My heart skipped a beat. It was exactly who I hoped it would be.

"Are you about to leave?" Brian asked.

I nodded. I was afraid to speak; afraid of what would come out of my mouth.

"So, I'll see you at school then . . ." he said.

"Yeah, definitely!" I said, a little too enthusiastically.

"High school is a big place. I'll be sure to keep an eye out for you, though," I added.

"Okay, me too," he said, with a slight smile.

I stepped in to give him a hug, one (I thought) he eagerly accepted. For a few seconds I felt the peaceful bliss that had made me so content the night before. The head on the shoulder, the hands on my back . . . it was completely comfortable. But it ended in hardly enough time for me to even begin to enjoy it.

"So I'll see you later, then," he said, and turned to leave.

"Yeah, later," I whispered. "Umm, Brian?" He stopped and turned his attention back to me. "If you want to . . . you know . . . umm, like . . . get together . . . or something . . . before school starts . . . just give me a call . . . I'll be around . . ." I stammered, my nerves trembling with anticipation.

He just looked at me standing in front of him, bright red and chewing my lips to death. Then he smiled, put his hand on my shoulder and said, "I'll keep that in mind."

After that, he turned and walked toward the parking lot. I watched his back get smaller and smaller until he disappeared behind a clump of trees. It was only then that I realized I was holding my breath.

Molly Gaebler

Fugue

A very small degree of hope is sufficient to cause the birth of love.

Stendhal

Let's call her Monique. Her real name always seemed too common for her, too plain. She moved to south Texas during our senior year of high school. She had transferred from somewhere up north, maybe New York.

Just as she was too grand for her small name, she was too lovely, too classy for our high school. She liked yoga and Mozart, wrote poetry and preferred old movies to sitcoms. She couldn't pass a bookstore or antique shop without browsing for an hour. But her parents had money, gobs of it, so the clique of similarly wealthy, popular students sucked her in, claiming her as one of its own before she could do anything about it. These were cheerleaders and athletes, blond-haired and well-dressed, who drove convertibles and finagled beer kegs for the parties they threw when their parents went on ocean cruises.

I was never invited to the parties. Whereas Monique preferred books over beers, I preferred skateboarding to school spirit. My hair was long, and my clothes were baggy. While the popular kids didn't hate me—at times it seemed to be strangely "cool" to be seen talking to a skater or surfer—they certainly didn't embrace me. My parents could barely afford to pay our bills, let alone go on a cruise. I spent my nights tearing around parking lots on my board. Occasionally, I'd see a car full of athletes and cheerleaders buying provisions for their parties. All of them looked so beautiful, wearing pressed shirts and perfume I could smell from across the parking lot. Sometimes they'd wave to me, as if a dangerous river raged between us, one that would drown them if they came any closer.

Monique sat beside me in English class, and in the course of the school year we became friends. That is, that's what she said we were—friends—when I or anyone asked. And as we spent more and more time together, more and more people asked. We went to lunch together—she drove us for sushi or Indian food (I'd never had such meals before) in her white convertible VW Beetle. We studied for tests at the library, and spent days and even a couple of evenings at the beach. My nights skating in abandoned parking lots dwindled. Once we snuck into a club and listened to a live jazz band. I've always remembered it was called Fugue. Monique told me their name came from Bach's *Toccata and Fugue,* and that fugue basically meant different instruments or voices coming together, overlapping and finally harmonizing. We saw movies, and I noticed that when she was scared she chewed her thumbnail. Sometimes she held my hand or kissed my cheek good night. Sometimes we held each other's gaze for a second too long. I adored spending time with her, and when I stood near her, my nerves fluttered, and waves of joy and panic rolled in my stomach. Somewhere between English class and California rolls, I'd fallen in love with her.

And so, apparently, had Paul Williams, a beefy line-backer. When they started dating, she told me about him as if I should be thrilled. Fool that I was, I pretended to be. Monique and I still went for sushi—Paul didn't share our lunch period—and for a while she made an effort to study with me or go to movies, but our time together started to fade. When we talked, the word "friends" came up more than it had before, as if she were defining our boundaries, and I began to hate it. Less and less, she reached for my hand, and she stopped kissing my cheek good night. It felt as if those parts of my body had vanished or been amputated; if she no longer touched them, they no longer existed.

So I returned to the darkened parking lots. I began to see Monique in the overloaded cars making their beer runs—though she never drank, or hadn't when we spent time together—and always Paul Williams was attached to her. She started calling me less often, even when she'd promised to, and some nights I picked up the phone and listened for a dial tone, hoping the problem was beyond her control. The phone, though, functioned perfectly. The problem was Paul Williams. They walked arm in arm wherever they went and kissed each other before tardy bells at school.

One day after English class, I blew up at her. I told her she deserved more than the big oaf, that he didn't understand her and she should open her eyes. I said she was changing for the worst, becoming someone I no longer recognized, and if she wanted to be part of a group who cared more about partying than people, we couldn't be friends anymore. (I'd rehearsed the speech numerous times in the mirror and in the parking lots.) Her face crumpled and turned red, tears hung on her eyelashes, and just as I was building to the part about how much I loved her, she spun and ran away. I don't know where she went, but I've always imagined she ran straight into the arms of Paul Williams.

We stopped speaking. I heard that she went to the prom with Paul and that she'd been accepted to Yale for the fall. As our graduation neared, I tried to say hello to her, to ask how she was doing and eventually to apologize, but she never responded. It was as if I were talking to myself in the mirror.

So on the night her little white car pulled into the parking lot where I was skateboarding, I expected it to park near the store and for Paul Williams to jump out and run inside. But the VW steered away from the store and pulled up to where I was trying to learn a new trick. Monique was alone, and when she approached me I expected her to scream and slap me, then to speed away into the night. That's what I deserved.

But for a while she didn't say anything. She just stood beside her car with her arms crossed. She looked at her feet, occasionally biting her thumbnail.

"You were right," she said finally.

"I was?" I didn't know what I'd been right about. My stomach tightened.

"I've changed," she said.

"What do you mean?"

"We can't be friends anymore."

I didn't know what to say. I realized I'd always hoped she would prove me wrong on that point. I'd only said it so she would prove me wrong.

And just as I was about to respond—I didn't know what I was going to say; I hadn't rehearsed anything— she started toward me. *Here it comes,* I thought, *the slap.* She walked slowly, still looking at the ground more than me, and without realizing it, she crossed the river that had always separated me and the popular kids, the river that had, for the last few months, separated me and

Monique. I braced myself and closed my eyes.

She kissed me. Her lips were soft and warm, but somehow they made me feel pleasantly cold. It took everything I had not to shiver. We kissed for a moment, and I didn't know what to do with my hands. I would learn. Before she left for college and we lost track of each other forever, Monique would spend the summer teaching me about love and friendship, showing me the strange and sad and occasionally beautiful ways the two complement each other or cancel one another out.

Don Keys

Just One Look, That's All It Took

My cousin was getting married, and I was tapped to be a participant in the wedding—a groomsman to be exact. Needless to say, I was pretty excited. My cousin lived in California and I lived in Washington, but since my cousin and I were very close, my family and I knew we had to be there for the wedding.

It was a gorgeous fall day in California, a perfect day for a wedding. The church was beautifully decorated and colors danced all over the room as the sun shone through the stained-glass windows. I looked as fashionable as ever in my black tux and emerald green vest. The bride was stunning. I never saw two people more happy just to be in each other's presence than I did that day standing at the altar. You could see in their eyes that this was true love. They had each found their other half.

I couldn't help but think about my relationship at home. As much as I wanted to deny it, it was falling apart. She was my first serious girlfriend. I loved her a lot, but when you start to forget the reasons why you got together in the first place and when the negatives start outnumbering the positives, it's time to say good-bye. I wasn't excited to go back home, to say the least, but my family had other obligations so we had to leave the following day.

Our plane left Los Angeles at 4:00 P.M. the next day. We had a two-hour layover in Seattle. My parents have a tradition of visiting the gift shops before flights. I decided I would stay at the boarding gate and do some homework. I started to pull out my math book when I looked up and saw HER. I couldn't believe my eyes.

She had on black sandals, black Capri pants and a yellow tank top. She was sitting in the seat across from me reading a book on the Holocaust. Her shiny black hair hung down over her face and, when she brushed it back, I got a true glimpse of her beauty. I was completely entranced before she even knew I existed. I had to say something; I couldn't let this go. How often does an opportunity like this come along? So I decided to introduce myself. I stood up and started to walk toward her. As I got closer, I realized that I wasn't ready to talk to her yet. I had no idea of what to say or how to say it, so I walked right by her and straight into the bathroom. Yes, I know, smooth. After I conquered my nervousness, I walked up to the mirror and practiced. Yes, I practiced—and all you guys out there know exactly what I'm talking about. I looked in the mirror and went through every single possible way of introducing myself to her. *Hello . . . Hey . . . How's it goin'? . . . Haven't I seen you somewhere before?* I left the bathroom and, as I walked by her again, I paused then sat back down.

Finally, a breakthrough. It just so happened that when I looked up at her again, she was looking back. Our eyes connected. A warm feeling covered my body. Not a sweaty warmth, but an inner warmth that was beyond comparison. It was more than just a look; we made a connection, and I didn't even know her name.

Something had to be done. I mustered up enough

courage to casually look over at her luggage, which was under her chair, to see if I could read her name and where she was from.

Then, the worst possible thing that could happen in a situation like this happened. Her plane was leaving, and I had to do something. She started gathering up all her things, and I started to panic. This could be something special, and I was in jeopardy of letting it slip through my fingers. Then, all of a sudden, she stopped. She pulled out a piece of paper from her planner and started to write something. She stood up, walked over to me, handed me the piece of paper and left without a word. Written on it was, "Just in case you ever get bored," followed by her address.

You know that feeling of complete and utter shock that you can't even speak? Triple it, and that was me. I had no idea of what to do next. She had walked to her gate, and I was left wide-mouthed and speechless. No way was I going to let it end there, so I stood up and ran to the gate from where she was leaving. When I got there, she had just handed in her boarding pass and was walking down the ramp. I prayed and prayed for her to turn around, just once, to see me, but all I saw was the back of her head going down the ramp to the plane. She was gone.

Back home, my relationship with my girlfriend eventually fizzled out. I got a handle on my life again and, exactly one month after the encounter at the airport, I wrote her a letter hoping she would remember me. I got a letter back from her almost immediately saying not only did she remember me, but that she had hoped every day for a letter from me in her mailbox.

We are now celebrating our six-month anniversary. The connection I made that afternoon at the airport was more than just a guy being attracted to a girl. It was a connection of souls, much as my cousin's was. We've had so many fun memories together, and we have plans for many more. Love found me that amazing day in September. It found my tired, doubtful self waiting at Gate C2D.

Dan Mulhausen

Friends for Life

Tim left for college on a Saturday and I on a Sunday. It would be the first time we had ever been apart over the course of our high-school friendship. Ours was more than a normal boy/girl friendship, though. Our close connection was the envy of others. I was in awe of his amazing personality, his hilarious jokes and his little-boy looks. He could read my mind, finish my sentences and bring me to hysterical laughter with only a look. We adored each other. As our last summer together approached, our bond only grew.

The summer started off slowly, with Tim trying to get my mind off the jerk I now refer to as my ex-boyfriend and a total waste of my time. Tim was dating one of my close friends and had been for a couple of months. I had to sit by and watch as she ridiculed him, made a joke of him in front of our friends, and eventually made him cry when she finally ended it. She broke my best friend's heart, and I ached with him.

We spent hours talking on the phone late at night, comforting each other, giving each other advice and worrying about college. Over the rest of the summer, both of us were single, so we spent all of our time together. Late at night after work, we would meet at cafés and just talk for hours. We grew even closer that summer. I only wondered why our friendship had to get so close now, as we were both preparing to leave for college.

As the time approached when we would have to say good-bye, we went shopping together for school supplies and planned our first rendezvous as college students for a month after we were both at school.

As I left that Saturday morning to take him to school, I was extremely nervous, my stomach full of knots. I kept wondering what was wrong with me during the three-hour car ride. Of course I was going to miss him, but this was not a sad feeling—this was nervousness. As we finished packing him into his tiny room and making it feel like some semblance of home, it hit me—and it hit me hard. I was in love with this guy! And it wasn't the friendship kind of love that I had felt for him throughout high school; it was something much deeper. I felt helpless. I had finally realized my true feelings for my best friend when it was too late. Tears filled my eyes as I sat on his springy, steel bed. I said good-bye to my best friend—and the love of my life—wondering if we were really going to meet in a month as planned.

That night at home as I packed my stuff I cried, scared that things would never be the same. We were both going to have our separate lives and would probably barely think of each other. Just then the phone rang, and as I wiped my tears and tried to utter a quiet hello, the voice on the other end let me know everything was going to be okay. It was Tim. Before even saying hello he blurted out, "Tina, we are going to have to make that rendezvous earlier than I thought. How about tonight?"

I was grinning like crazy as I practically hung up on him, jumped in my car without directions and headed for his school. How I got there in such a short time (an hour and forty-five minutes) is irrelevant. What is relevant is that the second I got there, I hugged him and told him I loved him. I had actually done that numerous times before, but this time he pulled away from my embrace, looked into my eyes, told me he loved me, too—and then kissed me. It was a kiss that seemed to contain months, even years, worth of love for each other.

When I left for school the next morning, I had Tim on my mind and in my heart. As I picked up my wallet to get money out to pay for a Coke, a tiny piece of paper fell out. It was from Tim and contained words that touch my heart to this day and still make me smile. "Tina, I am so mad at myself for waiting to tell you . . . I love you!" My eyes welled up with tears, and I felt truly happy and at ease with our situation.

I still keep that note from Tim, and we continue to share a remarkable friendship and always will. Only these days we also share much more—three beautiful children and the same last name.

Tina Leeds

Impossible Things Can Happen

It is not in the stars to hold our destiny but in ourselves.

William Shakespeare

Some guys in high school are "all that." They have everything going for them; they hang out with all the right people; they have all the good looks; they are so popular they have half the girl population in the school drooling over them; and they are totally unreachable. In so many words, that is how I would categorize Eddie. He had a great body, he was cool and I loved everything about him. I loved the way he made me feel every time he walked by. Most of all, I loved his bright brown eyes. He was perfect. I had a huge crush on him the moment I saw him but, of course, that was all he would be to me. A crush. I had always been this regular girl who just hung out with my friends during lunch, pretending not to care about anything but secretly glancing in his direction every now and then. He had always been the guy everybody knew and respected. Compared to him, I felt like I was insignificant.

My best friend, Angela, knew everything about my

secret crush on him, and she would never fail to remind me that we were not meant to be. In fact, she would remind me, if people knew that I had a crush on him they would probably laugh their brains out. It was like I was this commoner with a huge crush on my king.

Although we were never formally introduced, somehow our paths crossed. He talked to me one day when we were both late for school. He said hi and asked me why I was late. Naturally, I pretended to be unaffected and answered him right back. After that, I headed to my class. I was happy. He had recognized me as a living, breathing object that went to the same school. If I were a gymnast, I would have done several back flips just to release this flying feeling in my chest. I mean, I already felt shivers up my spine every time I saw him. So when he spoke to me it felt like someone had just poured a glass of cold water on my head.

After that incident, we casually chatted when we would see each other during lunch. Nothing personal, just some small talk that would last for a minute or two. Although we were talking and all, I could never imagine myself being his girlfriend. Pigs would fly before anything like that would ever happen to me.

One day, Angela's cousin from abroad came to visit her. She would be staying with Angela for a week. Her name was Tasha. We were introduced, and I liked her immediately. She was nice, funny, totally cool and a model back home. She had beautiful blue eyes and, well, I just had eyes. There was nothing to hate about her. Angela and I both loved hanging out with her so much that I finally suggested that she join us in school one time. Unknowingly, I initiated my own suffering.

When we went to school with her the next day, everybody was looking. She had those foreign looks and, well, she was a model. Everything was fine until she saw Eddie.

Guess what? She decided that she had a crush on him, too. Worse, she wanted to date him. She asked me to introduce them. I felt I had no other choice. I introduced them and told Eddie that she wanted to go out with him. To my disgust, he willingly agreed. I could have strangled myself.

So they went out, and I found out the next day that they had kissed. I can still feel the stabbing feeling in my chest when I found out. I couldn't believe that "my guy" was with this girl who liked him for just a second when I had been dreaming of him forever. It was unfair that she got to kiss him, and I didn't even get to tell him how I felt. I was too hurt to cry.

The day Tasha was leaving to go back home, Angela decided to stay at home and spend some time with her. I went to school. At the end of the day, Eddie approached me and asked if I could take him over to see Tasha before she left. After some persuasion, I finally gave in. But he would not be delivered to my rival without a cost. I got in his car and gave him directions to Angela's house, making sure he took the longest way possible to get there. When we were nearing the house I pretended to be lost, and I led him around in circles until he almost ran out of gas.

After talking and hugging and saying good-bye to Tasha (although I liked her a lot, I was secretly glad to see her go), it was time for us to leave. Eddie offered to take me home, and this time I gave him better directions. What a lame way to get even.

After Tasha left, Eddie and I were closer. We would go out sometimes and share more than just small talk. He would even join us for lunch sometimes. I now know why he was so popular. He was incredibly nice and absolutely fun to be with. I found myself falling for him more and more each day. Several times I wanted to let him know that I, too, wanted to date him. Maybe I would get a kiss, too.

One day he asked Angela and me to go to the mall. Angela never showed up so Eddie and I hung out by ourselves. I was overwhelmed. Deep inside I was thanking Angela for not making it. It was almost like a date, only he didn't know it. He asked me if I wanted to see a movie. I said yes. My heart was pounding. I swear he could hear it as we sat beside each other. I couldn't help but think of what it would be like if he knew that I liked him. I felt so strongly about him, and something inside me felt like he had to know. Since words are always so awkward for me, I decided that I wouldn't tell him; I would just kiss him. I gathered up all my strength and took a deep breath. I leaned on him a little, and he didn't seem to mind. I slowly faced him to plant my trembling lips on his cheek. When I looked at him, I was surprised that he was looking at me, too. I was so nervous, I could have choked on my own tongue. Then suddenly, *he* kissed *me.* I must have looked really stupid because I had my eyes open the entire time. I was in heaven.

I found out later that Eddie had liked me even before he met Tasha. He admitted to me that he never had the courage to let me know because he never thought I would like him, especially after I had introduced him to Tasha. Eddie and I have been together for almost four years now, and everything is still like brand-new. Not bad for two people who thought they would never be together. Surely, impossible things do happen.

Pegah Vaghaye

You Are All of This to Me

You're the thought that starts each morning,
the conclusion to each day.
You are in all that I do,
and everything I say.

You're the smile on my face,
the twinkle in my eye.
The warmth inside my heart,
the fullness in my life.

You're the hand that's laced in mine,
and the coat upon my back.
My friend, my love,
my shoulder to lean on.

You're my silly, mature, caring,
thoughtful, bright and honest guy.
The one who holds me tightly,
when I need to cry.

You're the dimple in my cheek,
the ever-constant tingle in my soul.
The voice that makes me weak,
the happiness of my life.

You are all I've wanted,
you are all I need.
You are all I've dreamed of,
you are all of this to me.

Melissa Collette

Lucky

*I've found that luck is quite predictable.
If you want more luck, take more chances.*

Brian Tracy

My crush could have been the perfect boyfriend if I'd let him. He wasn't what most people would call cute, but I didn't care. I had a gigantic crush on him. My friends called me "obsessed." I preferred the word "infatuated."

I'm not sure why I never told him. The worst he could have done was say, "Yuck." But in my opinion, that's not so bad. You see, I'm pretty darn vocal; I say it how it is. Except when it comes to boys. If there is a hot guy anywhere close to me, I completely clam up. My voice goes quiet and a bit squeaky, my hands slap together in a twisted glob, and I practically bite my lip off, not to mention I can only look at the floor.

When it came to my crush, it was the same. I was petrified. I was so worried about rejection, embarrassment and looking like an idiot, I didn't even consider a positive outcome. I couldn't see the doughnut itself, only that there was a hole.

When I heard the news that he was moving away, I was devastated. His dad, who was a doctor, had taken a job in another city. He told me that he might be coming back in the summer. But by summer, he meant July, and it was now only October. It was much too long to wait. I had to tell him. Maybe he'd try and figure out a way to stay.

Over the next few weeks, I tried to build up my nerve. I prepared to tell him that I liked him. I made up a gazillion scenarios, a billion different conversations, and a trillion ways to tell him my big secret. I played them over and over in my mind, scripting every word, every moment and action. I finally decided to tell him at the surprise good-bye party we were throwing for him. I would expose everything, including my feelings for him. Scary.

The party would have been fun if I hadn't been so nervous. I put on my happy face, trying to hide the fact that I was depressed. There were so many times when I wanted to tell him how I felt, but my brain always came up with a good excuse not to. Finally, as he was about to leave, I took a deep breath, walked up to him and said, "Peter?" I was surprised he heard me. I was so quiet, I could hardly hear myself.

"Yeah, Ambrosia?"

"Uh, um, I, I, I'm, I'm going to miss you," I stammered, hugging him with all my might.

"I'm going to miss you, too," he whispered, hugging me back. Then he turned and walked out the door with what looked like a little tear streaming down his cheek.

For the next few days, I moped around with little to say. All of my friends seemed worried.

"What's wrong?" my best friend finally asked. After making her promise not to tell anyone, I told her about Peter. She looked surprised.

"Really?" she asked.

"Yep," I said, regretfully.

"Wow! He had a crush on you, too!" she screamed.

"No way. I don't believe you," I said quietly. I was floored.

"I'm serious! He was going to tell you the day he left, but I guess he chickened out," she said. "Kinda like you."

"Yeah. Kinda like me," I replied, smiling into the sun.

A few days later the phone rang, and my dad picked it up. He said it was my "boyfriend." I figured it was one of the guys from class wanting to get the homework assignment. But I figured wrong. It was Peter. My "secret" had leaked out to one of his buddies, and he wanted to know if it was true or not. I took a deep breath. "It's true," I said. I couldn't believe it. The words were so easy to say.

"I really like you, too," he said. I wanted to store his words in my ear forever.

That's when Peter and I became a couple. And I learned that although feelings can be scary, they can also be liberating, opening up new doors to happy endings.

Ambrosia Gilchrist

Two of Me

I never thought I'd find myself
the day that I found you.
Plans for only
one of me
are future plans for
two.
Soul mates in this universe
that make the world surreal.
For when I'd given up on dreams
you showed me love is real.
And now that all my love for you
will never cease to grow,
please take me in your loving arms
and never let me go.

Anne G. Fegely

What I Really Learned in World Geography

Life without love is like a tree without blossoms or fruit.

Kahlil Gibran

The heavyset, middle-aged teacher scrawled his name across the dusty chalkboard as I studied my new classmates that agonizing first day of school. I felt like a kindergartner again. In reality, I was much older and all too familiar with the mass chaos that comes around every August. There was something about my third-period class, however, that told me my life was about to take a dramatic turn.

At the age of sixteen, I was just beginning my junior year, which meant rigorous studies in advanced placement computer science, physics, precalculus and, well, world geography, a course I'd somehow missed taking as a freshman.

During my first few moments in the class, it was exactly what I had anticipated—freshman guys and girls leaping wildly from seat to seat, endlessly chattering about "how different it was from junior high."

Just as I was reluctantly preparing for a semester of childish pranks, the class suddenly became much more appealing.

"Hey, Rosalinda, you're in this class, too?" asked a boy's voice that grew louder as he approached the skinny, pig-tailed girl seated in front of me. From what I gathered, the girl was Rosalinda, and he was one of her freshman friends.

In my relatively short life, never had I been so intrigued by a person as I was when that boy walked through the doorway. At five feet, four inches and about 125 pounds, Ethan had an aura about him. His skin was smooth and very fair, almost gleaming. His hair was a rich shade of brown and shinier than most girls' locks, with subtle golden highlights and perfectly spaced spikes at the crown.

Ethan was not beautiful in the way that most teenage girls think of Leonardo DiCaprio or even one of those boy band singers; he was a true original. His eyes, blue like midnight in the country and green as a sparkling emerald lagoon, were like nothing I'd ever seen before. They were reminiscent of a baby's—wide-eyed, innocent and glowing.

From the very moment I laid eyes on him, I was drawn to examine his every move. Ethan may have been physically breathtaking, but his mannerisms fascinated me, as well.

I found Ethan's walk particularly amusing. He strutted with a seemingly intentional limp, as if one leg stretched just a millimeter or so longer than the other. His walk was almost funny, but only if you paid as close attention as I did. It certainly made him unique.

As the tranquil autumn days wore on and my fellow world geography students became better acquainted with one another, casual friendships developed within the confines of room 522, namely my own with Ethan.

Slowly but surely, I became familiar with the dynamics of the boy whom I'd only weeks before admired from afar. Ethan possessed a genuinely giving heart behind that endearingly quirky smile. Our conversations flowed like a smooth piano melody after weeks of rehearsal.

The moon vaguely shone in the darkening sky that late September evening when Ethan first called me from his house, which, as it turned out, was not too far from mine. My feelings for him were becoming stronger. I was on top of the world and feeling as if thousands of angels had lifted my heart into the clouds and fluttered their velvet-soft wings against its glimmering surface. For the first time in my life, I felt an incredible surge of energy pulsating throughout my body. Something amazing was happening to me.

Ethan wasn't like any boy I'd ever known. The way he dressed (like every day was a special occasion), the way he laughed (like a clown who's had too much sugar), even the awkward way he pronounced his words were all his own. Everything I learned about Ethan made me twice as anxious to learn something else.

Establishing a relationship, however, would not be so simple. Our age difference of one year, seven months and thirteen days was magnified about thirty times in the eyes of our judgmental classmates. A junior girl dating a freshman guy was unprecedented and utterly incomprehensible, especially since my favorite pair of sneakers put me about a half-inch taller than him. For some reason, such details never seemed to interfere with Ethan's adoration for me.

Every day I debated the significance of those details, and every day I remained indecisive. I pursued an answer for nearly two months, continually asking myself if outward appearance and age actually overpowered real, true emotions. Ethan just listened as I poured out my fears over the phone, sometimes late at night.

The moment of truth came after Thanksgiving. I had spent the holiday at home with only my cat and a collection of my favorite television shows on tape. Ethan celebrated the holiday with his family at an uncle's house, somewhere up north. He was out of town for nearly a week. Never before did I realize what missing a person truly felt like. Along with everything Ethan had become in my heart, he was also my best friend. A part of me felt as if it had drifted off into space, leaving only a cold, sore wound when he was away.

I remember how delighted I was to hear the first tones of his voice when he returned home late Sunday night. I was so happy, in fact, that all of my doubts about the potential for a relationship had dissolved into thin air. Finally, I was ready to accept my feelings for him with open arms, and he reciprocated.

Like even the happiest of couples, Ethan and I were not without our troubles, but I was rewarded in ways I never knew possible when I was with him. Ethan taught me the power of courage, trust and, most importantly, that what lies in the heart exceeds all else.

Cortney Martin

I Finally Did It

If you play it safe in life, you've decided that you don't want to grow anymore.

Shirley Hufstedler

It was the last day of school of my sophomore year. I had just finished my English final, and everyone else in my class was exchanging their yearbooks to be signed. That's when he walked over—Jason, the six-foot-two, 175-pound, blond-haired, brown-eyed, mega-hottie, varsity football player, who I had been crushing on for four years. He came over to the girl I was sitting next to and asked her to sign his yearbook. He gave her his yearbook and went to the other side of the room to talk to some of his friends. When she finished writing, I asked her if I could have his yearbook. She agreed and handed it over. There I sat with Jason's yearbook. What was I going to write? Where would I even begin? I was shaking, and I could feel my face turning red. Whatever I was going to write, I had to do so quickly. I picked up my pen and started writing:

Dear Jason,

Another year has gone by. A chapter in our lives has come to an end and another one is about to begin. I guess now would be as good a time as any to tell you that I've had a crush on you since the seventh grade. I've been to almost all of your football games, and I've caught myself many times over the past few years staring at you in the hallways and in class more than one should. I think you are a wonderful person.

Love,
Katherine

Maybe it wasn't exactly that word-for-word, but it was pretty close. When Jason came back to get his yearbook, he had to ask who had it since the girl he left it with no longer did. This was my chance to talk to him and tell him I had it. When I did, he got this strange look on his face. I handed him his yearbook, and he went back to his desk. I watched him open the yearbook to where the girl sitting next to me had written. He read it then turned the page. My heart started pounding because I knew that was the page I had written on. He turned his yearbook to the side, and I knew then that he was reading my message. As he read his half-smile gave way to a full grin. I had no idea what to make of it. Was it good he was smiling? I think he was surprised that I had a crush on him, but I wasn't sure if he even cared. I guess I thought it was pretty obvious that I liked him.

Ever since middle school I would get all flustered and blush every time he was near me. In eighth grade during math class, he asked me once if he could borrow a pencil. When I got that pencil back, I treasured it and held on to it for a year or so, until I lost it. Then at eighth-grade graduation, my friend was trying to get her camera to work and she accidentally took a picture. Coincidentally, when she got her film developed, it was Jason she had accidentally taken a picture of. I took it home and framed it. In ninth grade he borrowed my calculator and I know it's crazy, but he left a fingerprint on it, and I was extremely careful not to wipe it off. It stayed there for a good few months until I finally came to my senses and realized how insane I was acting.

Jason finally closed his yearbook, picked it up and went over to one of his friends. He said something to him, and then they both slipped out of the classroom with Jason's yearbook. I realized I should have written "for your eyes only" in big red letters in hopes he wouldn't share it with others. But that probably wouldn't have worked anyway. I had a feeling he was showing his friend. Was it all a big joke to him? Or could it have been that he was truly touched by my sincerity and flattered by my words?

Jason and his friend came back into the classroom but not to stay. He rounded up some other friends and went back outside with, yes, his yearbook. A few minutes later the bell rang. Jason and all of his friends returned to the classroom to get their things. I didn't talk to him after that, and he never said anything more to me. Honestly, though, I wasn't really expecting anything to happen between us. I had placed Jason on a pedestal in middle school and never took him down. To me, he was the type of guy a girl like me could only dream about. For the past four years I had wished on every star, birthday candle and wishing well that we would be high-school sweethearts. I had laughed at his jokes and felt bad when he got hurt. But that day as I walked out of the classroom and shut the door behind me, I felt a sense of pride even after what had happened. I took a chance and told him how I felt. Even though it didn't turn out like a fairy tale—happily ever after—I was glad I did it. I felt closure, relief and satisfaction. I was able to put it behind me and move on. All of those years I had kept it inside, wondering "what if?" and being too scared to take a chance. I wasn't left wondering anymore. Now I knew.

Katherine Rowe

"I'll never forget my first crush. It was 75 years ago . . .
and I still haven't found the courage to talk to her!"

And There He Was

And there he was,
Staring into my eyes as a child stares at candy.
He was an image of perfection.
His sea blue eyes were as deep as the ocean,
And, oh, so full of mystery, like a treasure waiting to be
    opened.
He could win any girl's heart,
But he was awaiting *my* response to the question.
My stomach was churning like milk in a blender.
My heart was beating as if I had just run a marathon.
I was so excited that he had asked me,
Not just any girl, but me.
All I had to do was get the words out,
But it was hard.
His perfection stunned my thoughts,
Yet I managed to reply in a cool manner,
The words flowing off my lips as water flows through a
    stream.
"Sure, you can borrow my pencil."

Joanna Long

My Secret in Silence

You came into my life
Quietly, simply, placidly
And my words stood still . . .

I couldn't express in words
Or even in simple gestures
The secret I kept in my heart.

So I loved in silence,
Admired you from a distance,
Dreamt of you from afar.

I wanted to say I love you . . .
I wanted to say I care.
But cowardly, maybe, you'll only laugh at me.

In silence then I will love you . . .
In silence then I will care . . .

Lorelei Pablo

Reflections

As I make my slow pilgrimage through the world, a certain sense of beautiful mystery seems to gather and grow.

A. C. Benson

I sat on the blanket next to Shawn, eating candy corn and staring into the fathoms of the night sky. The stars illuminated the field, casting reassuring shadows of the familiar soccer goalposts and the mighty oak that had resided there for the better part of five generations. The cool November breeze brushed my hair out of my eyes and rustled the leaves up above. Far away a car rumbled along a nearby road, but civilization itself seemed incomparable to the majesty of the stars. They blinked on and off, teasing us with their translucence and the illusion of distance.

The comforting silence was broken by our hushed conversation and rhythmic breathing. We felt the need to speak softly.

"Do you ever think how different things would be if just

one moment of your life had gone another way?" Shawn asked.

"All the time. Like if I had just let up for a few minutes in that soccer game. I never would have torn a ligament. Where would I be now? Somewhere with a lot less stress, probably."

"I wonder if things are meant to be somehow, or if there is any pattern or direction to what we do?"

The wind picked up a little, blowing a scrap of paper in aimless circles. I pulled the blanket closer around us and winced as my leg twisted. I thought of the knee injury I was struggling to overcome, and how my performance as an athlete wasn't what it used to be. My parents were disappointed in my slow rehabilitation, and that my goals for the soccer season could not be reached. The week ahead of me was going to be filled with make-up tests and assignments, and I had to baby-sit the kids next door on Monday and Tuesday. My neck muscles returned to their familiar crunched-up position, and several chilly minutes ticked by before I again could appreciate the landscape.

Overcome by the importance of the sky, our conversation might have seemed irrelevant. Instead, it matched in feeling and intensity the emotion of the heavens. I became overwhelmed by the need to tell this person who I really was, what I felt and thought and dreamed. I felt important to be the recipient of his similar pondering.

What do you think love is? Shawn wondered. It wasn't really a question directed at me; it was more a train of thought. "I think it's the way the night is always there, but sometimes gets overpowered by the sun. Maybe it's the way you hear music—or feel it, and it becomes the best way to describe yourself. The stars, the ocean, a sunset—is that what love is?"

I didn't have an answer yet, so I took his hand and was surprised at its warmth. His fingernails were short and a little rough at the corners. I traced my finger over one absentmindedly, until it got caught on my skin, and I pulled my hand away.

I realized quietly that love is giving up a part of yourself and allowing that part to be filled by someone else. It's when your heart feels bigger than your whole body, because it's filled with trust and confidence and appreciation of one other special person. It's being able to communicate without a word and forgive unconditionally.

His blue eyes looked into mine, and he lifted his arms and invited me against him. I didn't have to tell him what I thought love was; we already knew. I settled into that place of a boy's body where you are amazed how perfectly you fit against each other. I brushed his sandy hair back and let my eyes fall on the faded scar on his forehead. It was ivory colored and slightly raised to the touch. Perhaps it was the imperfection that made him perfect.

"What is this from?" I asked.

"When I was really young I tripped over my brother and slid down some stairs. I remember I cried for hours even though it was only one stitch. I avoided those stairs like the plague for days."

The thought of this strong, self-assured person next to me sobbing over a butterfly bandage seemed so intangible that I laughed.

The corner of his mouth pouted as he pointed his finger at me. "What, you never had any scary moments as a kid?"

"Oh, I did, don't worry. But they were always fear of the repercussions of losing my house key or kicking a soccer ball through the window."

We laughed together and thought about how a child's reality differed so much from where we were in life now and how altered reality might be later. I didn't fear time itself, though. Time could never change emotion, only shape it in patterns and circles.

I pushed my forehead against the scratchiness of his chin, wondering how his facial hair could have such deep undertones of red. He warmed the tip of my nose with his neck. An owl rushed past overhead.

By and by, the peace of the evening alone, as the waning moon watched over his shoulder, replenished both of us. The pressures of school and parents and other such high-school problems diminished in significance. We were both ready to return the privacy to its rightful owners—the stars, the November breeze and the oak's shadow. Slowly, I pocketed the rest of the candy corn, planning to save it for our next encounter. John folded up the blanket, more neatly than I would have bothered to and I held out my hand to him.

We hesitated when we reached the top of the hill and turned to survey the world we had just left. I was reassured to see it was still there; the crumpled paper caught in the swaying grass, and a few discarded candy corn under the oak looking like psychedelic acorns. I stole a glance at Shawn, who was still holding my hand, with his large fingers wrapped around my ring finger and its neighbor. Life's daily problems had paled in comparison to his gaze and the starlight. He was also gazing at me, and his eyes still revealed the secrets the stars had shared with us that night.

Paige Melillo

The Sound of Silence

*T*elling someone the truth is a loving act.

Mal Pancoast

There comes a time in a relationship when someone will "drop the L-word bomb," as they say, and in our five-month relationship, it was Micah who did the duty. "I love you," he said. "I love you, too," I answered back. The words fell like paint out of my mouth. They were unnatural and tasted funny: so easy to say, and yet they were like a tough steak and I was a vegetarian.

It was my senior year in high school. I was eager to break out of the silly little life I had awkwardly outgrown, and Micah was the sailor who could rescue me from my desert island of high-school kookiness. He did, I suppose, but it was more than that. He was like no one I had ever met. He treated me like I was the only girl in the world. If Cameron Diaz walked by, he wouldn't turn his head. I was all he needed and all he wanted. Everyone else was out of focus in his eyes while I was crystal clear. No one had ever loved me the way Micah had. No one else could convince me that, even after a wisdom-tooth operation, I was beautiful, and that I had a "lovely" voice as I belted out Guns and Roses' "Sweet Child of Mine."

When Micah first told me that he loved me, I froze. We were lying side-by-side under the stars on the sand of Moonlight Beach when it happened. I had been told "I love you" before, but Micah was the first person who really meant it with every strand of his being. I had heard of out-of-body experiences, but had never really understood how they could happen. At that moment, though, I could actually see myself stiffen and visualize my words tumbling out of my mouth. He smiled at me, and we kissed. That moment stayed with me for weeks; in fact, it's still with me in the archives of my memory. We exchanged "I love yous" like baseball cards. And within a couple of weeks, "I love you" became our universal language. "I love you" meant hello, good-bye, I'm sorry, I'm happy, kiss me and thanks for lunch. Those three little words, those eight little letters, could sum up just about anything. I said them without thinking or feeling. I forgot that there was actually supposed to be meaning behind them. And then one day I realized that, even though I loved Micah and knew that I *could* fall in love with him, I was not "in love" with him, not yet. I had to tell him. I had to stop the hollow words that became the bookends to our verbal communication.

We sat in the silence of his truck for what seemed like hours.

"I love you," he said.

Silence.

"Babe? I love you." His voice rose, and his eyes became question marks. The sound of silence filled the interior and slowly rose like smoke out the window.

"Listen, Micah," I said. "Don't say that. Please. I'm not ready. I can't say it back right now. I mean, I love you, I do, but I'm not in love with you. Please give me time. I want to mean it, I want to mean it with my whole heart, and right now—I don't. I'm sorry." I looked up at him, into those glass eyes, waiting for them to break.

He smiled softly and nodded.

"Okay," he said. "You're right. I know how I feel. I am in love with you, Becca, but you need to find out for yourself. You need to tell me without my saying it first." He reached over and kissed me on the forehead.

"No more hollow 'I love yous,'" he said. "No more reciprocation. This isn't 'monkey see, monkey do'!"

I agreed, thanking him for understanding, and we went on, acting more and saying less.

Three weeks later, we were at the movies when it happened. Suddenly, with great force, my heart was flattened against my chest like wallpaper. I looked over at him and I knew. He was the most beautiful thing I had ever seen. He was glowing. All those times he had looked at me as if I was the world, and now I sat overcome by his presence and the tingles that filled my body. He was alive, the enigma of all that was heartfelt, and at that moment I was in love with him.

I lifted my chin and slowly moved my lips against his ear.

"I love you," I said, and this time my words were soft like cotton. I could feel my heart echo as the words fell out into the darkness.

He turned, slowly, and with a tear in his eye answered back.

"I love you, too," he said, kissing me.

And for a long time, even if Brad Pitt walked by, I wouldn't turn my head.

Rebecca Woolf

In Love

This feeling overwhelms me
A swelling of the heart
I never truly thought I would be
This happy at the start.

You take me by the hand
And lead me by the heart
Over a beach of sand
Through the grasses that we part.

With you I let go
Of intuition and sound mind
My feelings I cannot help but show
To a person who is so kind.

You kiss my lips so tender
Embrace me through the night
To you I have surrendered
Myself so hold on tight.

So strongly you hold my hand
Whisper softly in my ear
I really feel that you understand
Everything you hear.

I lose myself in you
This close I have never been
These feelings are so new
To have a lover who is my friend.

Michelle LaNoce

$\overline{2}$

BREAKING UP

When love beckons you, follow him though his ways are hard and steep.

Kahlil Gilbran

Breathing

(inhale.)
tears begin to flood my face like a cup left under a
running faucet well after the water has reached the rim,
my heart leaping to my throat,
getting caught,
squeezing,
twisting,
tearing.
my throat contracting around the emotions that threaten
to leap up & out of my lips,
my stomach
rumbling,
wrestling,
knotting.
my hands quiver as I reach up to blot the tiny teardrops,
leaving footprints down my cheeks.
the path that awaits me
suddenly seems like a pilgrimage,
one foot,
next foot,
step,
step,

I see you.
(I see her.)
you smile.
I smile.
(she leaves.)
you ask how I am.
(I lie.)
I reply that I'm fine
(even though my heart has just crept up into my mouth &
is jumping up & down on my tongue like an Olympic
diver waiting to hit the water).
I want to say that I miss you,
let you know that every moment I'm awake I think of you.
I want you to know that I miss your arms,
your smile,
your lips.
I want you to know that
(I'm incomplete)
my body hurts,
my soul bleeds.
I ask how you are
(hoping against all hope that you'll tell me what I want to
    hear).
you reply,
(your answer not including that you miss me,
that you miss my arms, my lips, my touch).
my eyes attempt to strip you down to your soul
(searching for what I once knew so well).
they get lost,
(but find their way back to reality when
they graze over the [ever-fading] hickey, just above
the collar of the shirt she bought you).
my heart leaps off the end of my tongue,
wanting you to see the way you've hurt me
wanting you to hurt the same way.

it falls to the ground.
(she calls you.)
you hastily say good-bye,
(as you trot over to her)
stomping,
squishing,
mutilating
my vulnerable, fallen heart.
(not even pausing long enough to scrape it off the
bottom of your shoe, like a discarded piece of gum.)
she wraps her arms around your neck,
brings her lips to yours . . .
(your ears still turn red.)
people pass, as if I don't even exist.
(I want to cry, scream, shout.)
I want someone to find my heart,
bring it back,
piece it together.
I turn away,
hoping that one day it won't hurt
(as much)
and hoping that I will again be able to call you
and have you come over to me,
be able to buy you shirts that match your eyes,
(and leave the telltale hickey just above the collar)
and will still be able to make your ears turn red from the
friction of our lips.
I walk away,
knowing my heart will not follow.
(exhale.)

Michelle Siil

My Best Friend

Do it for love.

Sark

My teacher is at the front of the class babbling some mumbo jumbo about regression equations or deviation scores. I lost her about two minutes into class. My attention is focused on something else—something more important to me. As I get lost in the gold X's and the sparkle of the diamonds fastened around my wrist, I remember back to April. A time when I was happy. A time when life was "perfect."

April was when Kevin and I got together (again). We'd been dating since January. We'd spent every free minute we had with each other. After all, he'd been my best friend since seventh grade. If neither of us had athletic practice, we'd sit on his couch watching television, wrapped in each other's arms for hours. Then it'd be time for me to leave for a game or him to leave for work. Good-byes were always long. We never wanted to let go.

On April 20, things were the same as always. I had a softball game and the bus didn't leave until 3:45 P.M. We were on his couch, as usual, but something was different with him. I'd never seen him look at me the way he did. I didn't really think anything of it, though. He'd always played mind games with me. Saying good-bye seemed harder for him that day, too. I didn't know what was wrong, but I didn't have time to ask because I was going to be late. I drove like a bat out of you-know-where and got to school just as the team was boarding the bus. My coach yelled at me for a while, but I tuned him out. I couldn't understand why Kevin was acting so strangely.

We were getting closer to the fields when my cell phone rang. It was Kevin. He sounded fidgety or antsy about something and said he really needed to talk to me. He told me to stop by his house on my way home from the game. Of course, I did. I cared about him so much and if something was making him upset, I wanted to be there for him.

We won our game. I drove to Kevin's house. He was sitting in his driveway when I got there. He looked so worried. I wanted to ask him what was wrong. I wanted to know why he looked so lost and alone. Before I had a chance to ask him what was wrong, he came over and hugged me. We stood in his driveway for a good twenty minutes before he began to speak. He pulled away from me, but didn't break contact. He looked deep into my eyes. I can still hear the words in my head: "I love you. I've never loved anyone before. I thought I had. You proved me wrong. I never thought I could care about anybody this much. It's so new to me, and I'm so afraid that you don't care about me like that." Then the tears came. In the years that I'd known him, I had never seen him cry. I'd heard him cry once, but it only lasted a minute or two. Seeing the tears pour from his eyes broke my heart. I had loved him for a long time, but I never let my feelings out for fear of ruining what we had. I started crying, too. They weren't sad tears, though. They were tears of joy. My heart felt bigger than my body. We held each other for what felt like minutes, but turned out to be hours.

"Jayme?" My math teacher's voice interrupts my flashback.

"Yes, Mrs. Cooper?"

"Can you answer the question?"

"I think it's three."

"No. Anyone else?"

I drift back into my thoughts. It was June, the day before Father's Day. My family and I were leaving the next day. Nine days in Wyoming with my family, not exactly my idea of a great time. My best friend, the person who held my heart, would be on the opposite side of the country from me. If I ever had any doubts about his love for me, they were all dissolved that night. He cried when I left his house, then we were on the phone in tears together until I had to get ready to leave at five-thirty the next morning. I called him every day from Wyoming. He would cry and tell me how much he missed me. He had a countdown going. Every day he'd tell me, "Only seven more days until you're in my arms again." After a delayed flight and an overnight stay in Dallas due to a missed connection, I was finally with him again. For some reason, I expected him to look different. He looked exactly the same: the same caring eyes, the same arms that always held me tight, the same soft lips that kissed me so gently. . . .

Someone hits my arm and brings me back to the present. "Hey, got any paper?"

"No, sorry." I put my head down, hoping no one else would interrupt my visit to the past.

October 20. Our six-month anniversary. Usually, I was lucky to have a relationship last six days. We were sitting in his car before school. He gave me a card. I still remember every word it said: "Jayme, I love you because whenever you smile it really lights up your face. Because your laughter fills up a room and makes it a happier place. I love you because you hold me real tight and tell me you love me, too. I love you because there's no one else in the whole wide world like you. Reach under your seat. I love you lots! Love, Kev." I reached under the seat and there was a velvety black box. I was already fighting back tears when I opened it. In it was the most beautiful bracelet I'd ever seen. It had gold X's and little diamonds in between them that represented O's. He told me it stood for "hugs and kisses." I started bawling.

It is these tokens of his love for me that still get me choked up. I feel the tears welling up in my eyes. I have to stop thinking about it. I listen to the teacher's lecture and scribble down some notes. It's no use.

December 17, I was at his car after school. I tried to stay strong about it, but I couldn't stop sobbing. Couldn't he see how much he was hurting me? Couldn't he tell how much I loved him? Didn't he care? I know he cared because he was holding me and wouldn't leave me until I was okay. He didn't understand, though. It was going to take me a long time before I was okay. I was so lost. In front of me stood my best friend, my first true love, and I was losing it all. He didn't understand what he meant to me. He didn't know everything he was to me. Who was I supposed to go to? I'd been with him for almost a year. My friends weren't really there because I'd lost touch with them. He was the one I always went to with my problems. Now I was faced with the biggest one yet: a broken heart. And I had no one to turn to. I put on a fake smile. I pretended I was okay. Inside, I was dying. I had opened myself up to him and let him inside of my deepest thoughts and the darkest recesses of my heart, and he had ripped it out. I had given myself to him and he had taken the most important thing in my life away from me: him.

I can't fight back the tears anymore. I ask Mrs. Cooper if

I can go sit outside. Of course, she lets me. I sit on a bench and stare at the trees. A gentle breeze blows through them. My cheeks are stained with tears. I think about it all. What would I be if I had never gone through this? I would have missed the opportunity to love and be loved. Where would I be if I had never met him? Would I still be that shy girl with zero self-confidence who hid under a barrage of baggy clothes? I don't know. I'm glad I don't know.

Kevin is still my best friend. My walls are covered with pictures of the two of us, as are his. I still get teary-eyed whenever Tim McGraw's song "My Best Friend" comes on. Kevin used to sing it to me. He still does. I can never forget the experiences we have shared together. And I'll always be his "little munchkin."

Jayme Johnson

Teenage Love

He loves me . . . he loves me not . . .
Love starts as an insignificant seed.
A wishful prayer,
a tiny fire,
a playful giggle,
a rosy blush,
a risky wink,
or a kindly smile.

He loves me . . . he loves me not . . .
Friendship buds.
A tender understanding,
a growing warmth,
a gentle trust.

He loves me . . . he loves me not . . .
The bud opens its first petals to a pair of
sparkling eyes
which twinkle with a new
passion.
A passion that overcomes all sense
until finally
a risky chance is
taken.

He loves me . . . he loves me not . . .
The rose opens into a
beautiful, ruby blossom.
Everything else in the world becomes
lost in a crazy, wild nonsense
a happy oblivion of exhilaration
complete and total
joy.

A sweet, innocent kiss
in the moonlight
seals the mutual promises
of never-ending fidelity.
Cherish.
Honor.
Protect.
Forever . . . or until

The blossom wilts,
and the petals fade,
and the promises break,
but the memories
of sunlight and blue sky
remain fragrant
preserved in the petals
of sachets
stuffed in the back of your sock drawer
and your heart.

Molly Day

Always

Love does not begin and end the way we seem to think it does. Love is a battle; love is a war; love is a growing-up.

James Baldwin

"So can I ride my bike to your house tonight? Give me directions."

I laughed at Adam's childish request. "Ad, I live in Washington. It'll take you hours to get there!" I stared into his dark brown eyes, waiting for a response.

As I studied his face, a look of seriousness washed over him, and he answered, "You know, I'd do anything to see you. I love you, Amy Catalano." He started to sing our favorite Bon Jovi song, "Always." I blushed and lowered my eyes. This wasn't the first time Adam had confessed his love for me. He was always saying things like that. But tonight, as we sat across from each other in the crowded restaurant, was the first time I said it back and really meant it.

"I love you, too, Adam Baldwin." He smiled and grabbed my hand. My mind raced. What did I just say? Did I just tell him I loved him? His smile told me everything I needed to know.

The year that followed was filled with many ups and downs for us. I spent much of the time battling a serious bout of depression, and we began to drift apart due to my lack of interest in the world surrounding me. Despite my mental state, I thought of him often and still loved him more than anyone. But I knew that before I could be with him, I had to get better. I couldn't let the weight of my world rest on his shoulders, and mine, too. That just wasn't fair. My junior year of high school soon ended, and the summer brought relaxation and long-awaited happiness. The storm cloud that had been resting over me lifted, and I was myself again. I called Adam one hot August morning, and we talked for hours. Just as I was getting ready to hang up, he told me that he wanted to see me and invited me to go boating with him and his family that day. I agreed.

The forty-minute car ride to his house was spent daydreaming of our reunion. I couldn't wait to have him back in my life. My heart had felt so empty without him. I was still very lost in thought when my mom pulled into his driveway. My stomach was tied in knots. I felt like I was meeting him for the first time all over again. I rang the doorbell. I caught my breath as the door opened. And there he stood—my Adam.

Adam and I sat in the bow of the boat talking while his parents sat in the back. I looked out over the water and the wind whipped violently around my face, causing my long blonde hair to come loose from its messy braid.

"You're so beautiful," he suddenly said to me. I hadn't heard those words from him in so long. My heart pounded as I gave a shy "thanks." Then he said it, the one phrase that would change everything: "I don't know how I feel about you anymore, Amy." I sat in shock, staring out across the graying sky. *This can't be true,* I thought to myself. *This can't be happening.* I looked at him, hoping that he would laugh and say that it was all just a joke. But the serious look on his face proved that he wasn't joking. I knew from that moment on, nothing would be the same.

I was right.

We soon began fighting, which was very out of the ordinary for Adam and me. We had always gotten along so well. He started pushing me away when I tried to reconcile, saying things like, "People change. Feelings change. You just have to learn to live with that." I had never felt so hurt in all my life. What had I done wrong? I had given him all of me, and I thought he loved me, too. I felt as though the past two years had been nothing but lies. I was left without any reasons, wondering why I had lost him. I pored over his e-mails and notes, and cried for the memories that remained buried in my broken heart. The tears stung my cheeks as I remembered those terrible words. While he moved on, I just couldn't bear to let him go. He was my first love, the first and only boy I ever said those three precious words to. I couldn't forget. I was hurt, angry and lost. I wanted nothing more than to cry myself to sleep and never wake up.

That was almost a year ago. Although I've let go of all the hurt and sadness, I haven't forgotten. We may have been young, but we shared something most people wait a lifetime for. He showed me what it meant to love wholeheartedly. He never judged me. He loved me for the girl I was and made me feel beautiful even when I thought I wasn't. He changed my life in an incredible way, and for that I will always love him.

Amy Catalano

Living Without You

I keep looking in all the places,
Where you are supposed to be.
But I never seem to find you,
And you're all I long to see.

I just can't seem to understand,
What it was that changed your mind.
All this time I thought I knew you,
When really, I was blind.

But know that I do not hate you,
And I know I never will.
Because I cared about you then,
And I care about you still.

Even though you hurt me,
I can't seem to let you go.
But I will go on without you,
And I want to make sure you know.

It will take some time to mend,
The damage that you've done.
But broken hearts do heal,
That's where strength comes from.

For now, the tears may be falling,
And my thoughts keep circling to you.
But soon, things will get better,
If you have hope, then they always do.

Kristy Glassen

Late-Night Talk

His name came up
On the caller ID
At exactly
Eleven forty-three.

I answered it
In my cheery fashion
For our late-night talks
Were always my passion.

But his voice told me
That something was wrong
Like a horror movie's
Foreshadowing song.

As he took a deep breath
And told me the phrase
"We need to talk"
I was put in a daze.

"We have a connection
And get along fine
There's nothing you've done
The problem is mine.

"You understand, don't you?
Are you still there?"
I tried to answer
As I felt my heart tear.

"We're gonna stay friends,
We'll talk every day.
Nikki, do you have
Anything to say?"

A thousand thoughts were
Ready to spill
But my mouth wouldn't talk
As my eyes began to fill.

Thoughts raced through my head
Old memories played
The thought of being alone
Made me feel so afraid.

"I'm not expecting you
To understand.
You're a sophomore,
Life holds different demands.

"Still one day
When your life is SATs'
College applications
And activities,

"You'll realize why
I made this choice.
Talk to me, Nikki,
Do you have a voice?"

I would if I hadn't
Hung up so quick
To comfort myself,
I was feeling quite sick.

So then this is it,
This is the end.
What more can I say then?
I'll miss you, my friend.

Nicole Hamberger

The pressure of the SAT finally pushes
Brian Folbert over the edge.

The First

Plunge boldly into the thick of life.

Goethe

It ended as abruptly as it began. A brief phone call, then the final good-bye. I hung up the phone and sat silently in a daze for a moment. Then reality sank in, and I began to cry. A friendly breakup of a far-from-perfect relationship, and yet it still hurt. A lot.

It was in the school gym, among all our friends, that he began to weave his magic. It began with a sweet smile and a light brush of his fingers across my arm. A half-hour before the dance ended, he uttered the words I had been dying to hear:

"Want to go to a movie sometime?"

I responded with a calm smile and a confident "yes" that belied the excitement coursing through my body. I felt as though I had won the lottery. My life was now complete. I had a boyfriend.

We walked out to the parking lot together, and with his mother waiting in the car just out of sight, he gazed into my eyes and kissed me on the cheek. Then with a whispered promise to call, he left. It felt so unreal. In one night, we had gone from being mere acquaintances to being the closest of friends. We were a couple.

Soon, we were strolling down the halls hand-in-hand, and I could think of nothing but him. I was nuts about him. I had been eagerly awaiting the experience for what felt like forever—the special bond between first loves that is like no other, the closeness between a couple, and perhaps most of all, my first kiss.

It took four dates before it happened. Up until then, we had held hands and cuddled, sitting close together in the plush seats of a darkened movie theater. The cuddling was just as much fun as kissing turned out to be, if not better. He had this way of rubbing his thumb across my knuckles that gave me butterflies.

Finally, we kissed. I had always wondered what my first kiss would be like. One night his mom dropped me off at my house after a movie, and he walked me to my front door. We stood under the porch light, gazing at each other shyly. Then he slowly came toward me, lowered his head and kissed me. It was over before I even realized it had happened. I wish I could say that fireworks exploded, but they didn't. After all, it was only a two-second meeting of lips. Nonetheless, it was everything I had hoped for. It was sweet and tender and caring, and just the tiniest bit awkward, because it was his first kiss, too.

If only the rest of the relationship had progressed as wonderfully. Sure, we had many good times, but the true meaning of the word "relationship" was missing. He never seemed to notice, but I was miserable for much of the time. It's hard to put a finger on what exactly bothered me. Mostly, it was a whole lot of little things. We used to go to a movie every weekend without fail. That was fun, but I never got to choose what movie we saw. Also, we never did anything *but* go to movies. He didn't like going out to eat or even talking. Sure, we discussed movies and recent releases by our favorite bands, but that's about as deep as our conversations got.

Yet, it still didn't occur to me to break up with him. I don't know if it was him that I was so infatuated with or if I was in love with the fact that I had a "boyfriend." I can't deny the pride and confidence I felt when I walked down the street holding his hand and saw how the other girls eyed me enviously, attracted by his good looks and sweet smile. I don't know why I felt that having a boyfriend was so important or why I somehow used it to judge my self-worth.

Finally, I couldn't take it any longer and I became honest with myself. I wanted the relationship to improve or I wanted to move on. And I told him just that when I called him one Friday night. To my astonishment and disappointment, he responded by saying we'd be better off as friends. I agreed. I didn't say anything; I think I was shocked at how easy it was for him. After promising to stay friends, I hung up and it was over.

After the initial shock wore off, my first feeling was one of relief. I no longer had to wonder what he was thinking all the time or ponder where we stood. Then it hit me: It was over. I cried. And then I got mad at myself for letting him make me cry. I blamed myself for not making it work. I cried some more.

And then one day I woke up and realized that life goes on. I experienced a lot of firsts with him—my first kiss, my first love and even my first heartbreak—and I'm grateful for all of it.

Hannah Brandys

Another first date is ruined
by an embarrassing commercial.

One of Those Days

*For of all sad words of tongue or pen,
the saddest are these: "It might have been."*

John Greenleaf Whittier

Today is one of those days that I miss him—the lonely
I-wonder-what-he-is-doing days. I don't have them often,
hardly at all, but once in a while I do when I hear a song
he used to sing or drive past his neighborhood. I am not
sure why it is that I sometimes still miss him. It's been
nearly eight months since we broke up for the second
time. Maybe losing him bothers me a lot more than I let
myself believe. Sometimes, I hate myself because I know
that I am to blame.

The first time I met Justin I was completely infatuated
with him. I just knew that I had to be with him, and two
months later, I was. For a while, I thought my life was perfect. He was older and more mature than previous
boyfriends were; he knew how to have a real relationship
that meant something. I was always happy, and I always
felt beautiful around him.

Eventually, my immaturity began to surface. Three and

a half months into the relationship I started to feel like my freedom was dwindling. I still cared about him a lot, but I was feeling exhausted. I needed a break. He wasn't ready to let me go, but I wasn't going to let that stop me. Tearfully, I chose to take the road of independence and broke his heart in the process.

I dated other guys, but he would creep into my thoughts at least once a day. None of the guys measured up to him; none of them gave me the special feelings that I longed for day after day. Then, one day, about eight months after our breakup, he called out of the blue. Until then we had barely spoken, and I realized just how much I really missed him. We decided to get together and catch up. We went out to dinner, and he talked about his new girlfriend . . . a lot. I thought I was going to have to dump my glass of water on him to get him to shut up about her. After a long conversation he revealed that he wanted me back. And I wanted him back. So, after his breakup and a few more emotionally charged talks, we got back together. It almost felt as if no time had passed since we were last a couple. We were happy, and I felt complete again. I had matured a lot and could now handle committing to him. Sometimes my adoration for him would overwhelm me. Never before, and never after, have I cared about a boy so strongly.

After a while, though, I became too busy with my after-school activities to be able to put so much energy into the relationship. He felt like I was betraying everything that we had, everything we had worked for. And in a moment of anger, I felt like he betrayed my trust in the worst way. We broke up. I held a grudge for a long time. My pride was wounded and my feelings torn.

With time we were able to be friends again. We had given it two tries, and it seemed it wasn't meant to be. What I learned from him and the relationship was worth all the painful times we went through. There were many happy memories, too. I heard a quote once that rang loud and true: "You always believe your first love to be your last, and your last to be your first." For me, he's been both. We shared secrets and laughs, rainy nights and sunny days. Though we experienced many storms together, we taught each other valuable lessons about life and love. The way that I was able to look at myself through his eyes was one of the most amazing feelings I've ever had. But, there comes a time when the feelings start to fade and the memories become bittersweet. A time where all that you can do is hope that somehow he will realize what a difference he made in your life and how he contributed to the person that you've become.

I can't ignore the feelings that once were. I can, however, let go and remember.

Cassie Kirby

"I told you, it's over. You've got to forget about me!"

Reprinted by permission of Randy Glasbergen.

Sand Castles

She frantically piled sandpile on top of sandpile trying to build her dream sand castle independently, without her father's help. Finally, she gave up. With her silk pink ribbon hanging over one eye and sand building up inside her bathing suit, she ran over to her father.

"Daddy, I can't build my sand castle good enough. Help me!" she demanded.

Her dad scooped the sandy girl into his arms and, with a broad smile on his face, looked pleased that she wanted his help. He carried her over to a nice, flat spot of sand, and together they built a charming sand castle.

When they were finished, he took her tiny, sticky hand in his, and her puffy little fingers clung to his large firm hand. "I love you, Daddy," she said looking up at his face with large, expectant eyes.

"I love you very much, my little princess," he replied.

But then the huge majestic waves pulled at her feet like a rope tugging her into itself. She tried to break free from her father's protective hand so that she could play alongside the waves.

"Daddy, I want to go play in the ocean," she informed him.

"Okay, but I'll come with you to make sure the waves don't pull you away."

"No, Daddy. I want to go in by myself." And with that independent statement, she ran into the waves, which welcomed her with full force. They filled her senses with a pungent, salty smell, the foam blinded her eyes, and her active little body became one with the fast flowing water.

Twelve years later, the same girl, now a young woman, had lost her ribbons, but not her assertive independence. Her frilly, pink bathing suit had been reduced to a skimpy, green two-piece. Her long legs glided out of the harsh waves.

A young man with wavy golden hair flashed his magnetic smile at her, and her coy expression met his face. He wrapped her in a towel as he gazed into her deep, green eyes.

As they sat cuddling on the sandy beach, warming their feet in the thick pebbles, she asked him what he was thinking.

"Well, actually, I was just thinking that . . . never mind, it's deep. Let's just sit here," he said uneasily.

"Come on, what were you going to say?" she prodded him.

Her long, slim fingers had lost their puffy, childish features, and now they ran through his rough and wild hair as the wind played between the strands.

"It's kinda crazy. But, I think . . . I think . . . I love you," he replied.

Her eyes froze as she looked into his eyes. He looked down at the ground and nervously sifted the cold sand through his fingers.

"I don't know what to say," she truthfully told him.

"It's okay, you don't have to say anything."

A tear formed in her eye. She felt warm, and pleasure filled her heart.

Finally, they both got up, and she playfully kicked sand on his legs. He chased her down to the waves. As they landed on the cold, shifty ground, she said, "Let's make a sand castle like I used to do when I was little."

He looked at her with a funny expression on his face, but her enthusiasm enticed him to enter into his past. Together, they piled layers of sand on top of each other. But the waves kept claiming their fortress, blanketing the couple's efforts and stealing the sand back to its ocean floor.

Finally, the two of them lost interest in their failed efforts and walked back to the car, trudging their feet through the sinking sand.

After a few months, she came back to that same spot on the beach. This time, she was alone. Tears slept in her eyelids as resentment rested heavily in her heart. Her brain felt as though it had been filled with sand, and she could not think anymore. She felt dizzy and lonely. She thought of all the dances they had gone to, all the promises he pledged to her, and all the smiles she had thought were only flashed in her direction, although now she knew otherwise.

She collapsed her frail body on the hard and shifty sand. The pebbles were unusually cold as the clouds crawled along behind their mother sun. She desperately grabbed for the sand, for something to hold on to, but it seeped between her fingers. She began to unconsciously pile up sand. As a castle began to form, she decided it was a good idea to continue to build it; maybe it would take her mind off her sorrow.

Somehow, building the sand castle brought her a sense of peace. Something about it comforted her and began to make her feel like a child again. She felt innocent and lighthearted. The feeling of the sand in her hands and the strong scent of dried seaweed brought her back to a time when she was much younger, and life seemed simple.

She began to remember her failed attempt to build a sand castle when she was younger, her father's smile and his watery eyes filled with love as he helped her build her dream castle.

She struggled to push herself up from the suppressing sand and reached into her pocket for some change. She trudged to the pay phone as her toes wiggled in the wet sand that covered the concrete floor and made her feet unusually cold. Picking up the receiver, she dropped the coins into the slot and dialed the number she had known by heart since she was a little girl.

Her father picked up the phone almost immediately after the seventh digit had been pushed.

"Daddy . . . ?"

"Honey, is that you?" his voice sounded relieved.

"Dad, I just wanted to say . . . I love you."

There was a pause.

"I love you, too, my little princess."

As she walked back down the sand to get her shoes, she spotted her sand castle. The waves had not touched it. It stood strong above the rest of the sand, while the waves crashed in the distance.

Jennifer Reichert

When We Risk It All

We can't blame others when love dwindles away—
For we knew from the start it never promised to stay.

It's just one of those things where the stakes are high—
And sometimes it's forever, and sometimes it's good-bye.

When you love the right way, you will never lose—
No matter what path life may force you to choose.

You may end up with tears or a broken heart—
But you knew what you signed up for from the start.

You can only give what you've got to give—
And if that's not enough, then you must continue to live.

Life will go on and broken hearts will heal—
You must continue on your quest, for that's the deal.

Throw your heart into life and never stall—
For the greatest risk is to risk nothing at all.

You see, love is the only thing that we know—
That can be divided and divided but continue to grow.

And life isn't long enough to lock away our heart—
Just because life may have forced two people apart.

We will continue to love and continue to lose—
We will continue to pick and continue to choose.

And then one day we will just risk it all—
Take the chains off our hearts and dismantle the wall.

The last time we love will be the *forever*—
And never again will our hearts be forced to sever.

We'll never have doubts that it'll go away—
Because this time, it'll be here to stay.

But until then we must endure all the pain—
For we only see sunshine if we can wait through the rain.

Kristy Glassen

$\overline{3}$

FRIENDSHIP

*The supreme happiness of life is the conviction
that we are loved.*

Victor Hugo

Tinfoil and a Hair Ribbon

Not a letter, not a card, and not even a call.
How could Jane have forgotten, when they'd been
    through it all?
Teardrops and heartache, they'd shared many things,
Crushes on boys, their hopes and their dreams.

Haircuts and makeup and CDs and clothes
Secrets and habits, they even shared those.
So where could she be, didn't she care?
Why didn't Jane come, why wasn't she there?

Through the second grade, third grade, fourth grade, too,
The fifth, sixth and seventh, their friendship grew.
Always and forever, they vowed till the end
To faithfully be there, as the other's best friend.

And they always had been, even when Jane moved away.
But for whatever reason, she wasn't there on that day.
And Allie felt sad as she circled the crowd
As her graduation party grew increasingly loud.

And then she heard it, a loud knock on the door
As she quickly hurried across the bustling floor.
Weaving through family and friends without care
Hoping and praying, when she opened the door, that Jane
    would be there.

But there on the stoop was a deliveryman instead
In his hand was a package, addressed to Allie, he read.
She reached for the package and brought it inside
And as she tore open the cover, she started to cry.

For the package was wrapped in tinfoil, with a hair
    ribbon tied with great care
And a million memories came flooding back, as Allie stood
    tearfully there.
For Jane hadn't forgotten, and as a smile crossed her face
Allie's memories took her back to another place.

Many years prior when she and Jane were so young
When they joined the local Brownie troop all in great fun.
And Allie was so excited about the Christmas party her
    troop was to have
That she never noticed that Jane didn't seem quite as glad.

On the day of the party, everyone brought an unmarked
    gift, and numbers were drawn
And with anxious eyes, Allie and Jane both looked on.
At the table piled high with presents galore
Wrapped in beautiful paper and ribbons bought from the
    store.

But one particular gift seemed out of place and well
    hidden
For it was wrapped in tinfoil and tied with a worn-out
    hair ribbon.

"What kind of person would give a gift that's so lame?"
The girl who received it cried out in blame.

Tears stung Jane's eyes as the girl carried on
Complaining quite loudly how much she'd been
    wronged.
As her accusing eyes searched, looking at each girl all
    around
Jane shifted nervously and stared at the ground.

For inside the package was Jane's favorite bear
And the ribbon on the package, Jane had worn in her hair.
And because Jane lived with her grandma, and money
    was tight
She gave away her most treasured thing, because she felt
    it was right.

And just when Jane felt the presence of tears
She heard her friend Allie saying quite clear.
"I'll trade you," she said, as she offered her gift
Of nail polish and jewelry, all glamour and glitz.

"I've always loved bears, and that one is especially neat"
As she grabbed the bear from the girl and returned to her
    seat.
And it was then on that night, they each knew for all time
They'd found a true friend, a one-of-a-kind.

For Allie knew what it meant for Jane to give up that bear
And she knew how special the ribbon was that Jane once
    wore in her hair.
For Jane's mommy and daddy died when she was just
    five
And the bear and the ribbon helped to keep their memory
    alive.

For Jane's daddy had lovingly given his daughter that
    bear
And Jane's mommy had crocheted the ribbon to put in
    Jane's hair.
And so as the girls walked side by side together alone
Allie handed the bear and the ribbon back to Jane before
    they got home.

And no words had to be said, as they both started to cry
And then they each headed to their houses, waving
    good-bye.
Tears streaked down Allie's face, as she stared again at
    that old bear
And the crocheted ribbon Jane once wore in her hair.

And then with trembling hands, she retrieved from the
    box a handwritten note
And read over and over the words Jane had wrote.
"I'm sorry I couldn't be there, Allie, but Grandma is ill
Yet I wanted you to know that I think of you still
As my very best friend whom I always will love.

"And so with my bear and my ribbon, I send you a hug.
I should have called sooner, but I didn't want to dampen
    your day.
And I knew if I told you about Grandma, you would have
    hurried my way.
And I wanted your party to be all you deserve.
I'm still your best friend, Allie, you have my word."

Always and forever, they vowed till the end
To faithfully be there, as the other's best friend.
And as Allie held the ribbon and hugged that old bear
She knew Jane was the one friend who always would care.

And then Allie decided her best friend should not be
   alone
As she went to her bedroom and reached for the phone.

Cheryl Costello-Forshey

Saying Good-Bye

Today I said good-bye to my best friend—the one person I have been able to count on for so many years. She has been my companion through low self-esteem, hard tests and bad prom dates. She's someone who could finish my sentences, who never failed to understand me, yet whom I could talk to for hours on end. My friend when friends seemed scarce and life too hard. Who'd laugh with me at jokes no one else understood. Though it took me a while to realize that a best friend is more than a title or an old habit, she was always there.

High school flew by so quickly that I hardly knew what I always had in front of me until it was getting ready to end. Our last year together was spent with late-night outings to 7-Eleven and the playground or to the river. Exploring our small town convinced me that we could discover something for ourselves. The realization that her home had become another home to me, her family an extension of my own. College applications, tears of frustration and anger, AP Exams and SATs, and, hardest of all, sitting there in my cap and gown with my classmates, listening to her speech. My best friend: intelligent, president of the Student Council, funny, beautiful, amazing. She's someone I'm honored to lean over and whisper about to a classmate: "She's my best friend."

A friend who didn't have to ask, "Are we going out Friday night?" but instead, "So, what are we doing Friday?" Attached at the hip through disloyal people, bad dates, long nights spent studying. And now, because we are "old enough," we must head our separate ways—her on one side of the country, me on the other. Tears and discussion, excitement and fear for weeks beforehand. Last movies, dinners—the last everything. All this pain, and always putting the good-bye off until the last moment. Funny how, at the last moment, as I drove to her home this morning and hugged her for the last time for four months, the tears fell only for a few minutes. Because I've realized that it's not good-bye forever, just until again. We'll always have e-mail and phone calls, and Christmas, spring and summer breaks. When you have a once-in-a-lifetime friend, you're always together, no matter how much distance is between you. Real love stretches and bends; it does not see state lines.

Or maybe the reason the tears dried up and the sobs stopped wracking my body as I drove away from her house, seeing her wave until I was out of sight, is because I've realized how amazingly lucky I am to have someone who is so hard to say good-bye to.

Kathryn Litzenberger

I Hope

I hope you surf the waves in from the ocean,
big and small.
I hope you watch the sunset,
from a mountain straight and tall.

I hope you sing a song to all the angels,
loud and clear.
I hope you'll always try new things,
never giving in to fear.

I hope you fall in love,
with one who makes your world go 'round.
I hope that if you fall out,
your feet stay on the ground.

I hope that you can understand,
that true love waits for you.
That you may have to wait awhile,
but when it comes it will be true.

I hope you feel the sand,
hot on your toes on summer's day.
I hope you learn that sandals,
help to keep the pain away.

I hope you find a rainbow,
and realize it was worth the rain.
I hope that through your journey,
you'll learn to balance smiles with pain.

I hope that you will realize,
life isn't always on your side.
I hope you know when hope is lost,
in me you can confide.

I hope that your glowing smile,
brings someone out of gloom.
I hope you taste your life,
with more than just a spoon.

I hope that when you're lost,
you are also one to find.
And I hope that your hand,
never grows too big for mine.

I hope you watch the stars shoot by,
upon a grassy hill.
I hope you know I love you,
always have and always will.

Laura O'Neill

Losing My Best Friend

In a friend you find a second self.

Isabelle Norton

Tears streamed down my face as I hugged Kristen tightly. I whispered good-bye and got into the van to travel back home to Tennessee, which meant I would be leaving my best friend in the whole world hundreds of miles away at her new home in Texas. I didn't know how I would ever be able to deal with this terrible loss. As I left I clutched my favorite pillow close to me, wondering what my life would be like without Kristen in it. Trying to stop the pain I shut my eyes and let all the memories of joy I had shared with her slowly flow into my thoughts. Pictures of smiling faces and the sound of laughter played out in my head.

For six years we had shared every detail of our lives, big or small, with each other. We constantly helped each other deal with all the pain, suffering and joy that comes with the new experiences you face as a teenager. I depended on her for so many things, and she was unceasingly there for me. She always listened closely to my problems with a nonjudgmental ear and helped me solve them. When I desperately needed someone to laugh at my jokes and give me encouragement to follow my dreams, her words always reassured me. When I needed someone to help me understand why I cried because my heart was breaking, she simply cried with me. I shared every secret with her, causing me sometimes to wonder if she knew more about me than I did about myself. Being around Kristen helped me to learn who I was and who I wanted to be.

As I felt another teardrop roll slowly down my face, I was hit with the horrible memory of the night Kristen called me with the bad news.

"What? You have to move? Your dad is being transferred to Texas?" These questions tumbled out of my mouth. I felt myself panicking as my mind began to race, searching for some explanation that would help all of this make sense. Please, please let this be some cruel joke. I wanted to scream, but it was true. Kristen would be leaving in just a few months. I was devastated. This was one problem that we couldn't resolve. There was nothing either of us could do to change what was going to happen.

The memories of Kristen's farewell party flashed before me. Balloons, presents, food and friends filled the room. Kristen was opening her presents. As she opened mine, a photo album filled with pictures, I stood up to read her a poem I had written.

Remember Me Always

So many memories we've made together
As the years have slowly passed.
Tears may have been cried
But our laughter drowned them all out.
Sharing my deepest-most secrets

'Til one in the morning at your house.
Talking forever about things
Until our words just ran out.

But now you must leave,
And I stay behind.
Who will I call
When I just need to talk?
Who will you lean on
When your problems weigh you down?
Who will laugh at my jokes?
Who will make you smile?

I can't tell you the answers
To the questions I have.
But I want you to know
I will always love you as my friend.
And when your heart is troubled,
I want you to think of me.
Remember the times of joy
We have shared
And maybe it will make you smile.
And since you can't take me with you,
Take the memories we have made
And cherish them
As I always will.

I quickly pushed that memory aside, not wanting to relive the emotions written on everyone's faces as I read aloud. More images zipped through my head.

It was the week I traveled with her and her family to Texas. I remember sitting on Kristen's kitchen floor of her bare house waiting for the movers to finish packing some of the last belongings and feeling extremely lost. Once we arrived in Texas we stayed at a hotel for a few days while they moved into their new house. Kristen unpacked her keepsakes, placing everything down with care and asking me if it looked all right. No, of course it didn't. She wasn't supposed to be here and neither were any of her possessions. But I simply told her that it all looked fine. For the rest of the week, we went swimming and to the mall trying to make new memories that we could reminisce about later. We stayed up every night until the early morning hours just talking. Then the day came when I had to go back home. I wasn't going to relive that morning with all the tears and good-byes. I popped open my eyes, snapping myself back into reality.

That dreadful week happened almost two years ago, but the memories of it are as vivid as if it happened yesterday. Kristen and I call each other all the time and write each other every detail about our lives. Sometimes when I talk to her on the phone, I forget she's hundreds of miles away. She's still as large a part of my life as she was before and vice versa. Our friendship is so strong that it can face anything. I am very lucky. I've found my soul sister, and I am able to share my life with her. The distance just doesn't matter.

Amanda Russell

My Friend Andrea

Those who do not know how to weep with their whole heart don't know how to laugh either.

Golda Meir

I felt tears well up in my eyes as I heard my best friend's name called and watched her walk across the stage to receive her high-school diploma. She shook hands with the school-board president, had her tassel turned by the superintendent, and finally received her diploma from our principal. She stopped briefly to face the audience while they took pictures and applauded her. She was an honor student and first in her class. I felt a sense of pride and smiled to myself as flashback after flashback of our childhood paraded through my mind.

I remembered the winter that we decided to become bobsledders. We packed snow on the front steps of my house and let it set up overnight so we could sled down the icy strip on orange saucers at breathtaking speeds to the street that separated our houses. I relived the excitement of singing into our baking spoons about "rocking the town inside out" while sliding across the kitchen floor in our socked feet. One summer we both had Nickelodeon Moon Shoes. We would bounce all over Andrea's front yard and make music videos—without a video camera.

I had to suppress a laugh as I thought of the time that we lit a bonfire in our clubhouse that was located under my front steps. It was a normal summer day, and I was just hanging out in our clubhouse. As I looked around, I decided that we had too much garbage lying around and needed to dispose of it. Andrea came over in a flash and was more than willing to join the fun. We filled an ice-cream pail with water in case something should happen, then out came the matches. We put the garbage in a pile and lit it up. It got a little out of hand and started climbing the wall. Fortunately, we had the bucket of water and put it out before anything of importance caught on fire. Yep, we got in trouble for that little episode. The front entryway of my house smelled like a chimney, and when my parents caught a whiff they herded us in for a lecture.

We took a stab at writing songs and hosting our own talk shows. We dealt with important issues like what kind of shoes we were wearing and what our moms were making for supper on that particular night. We also addressed the fact that Mr. Freeze Popsicles were part of a balanced diet and should be included in one of the major food groups. Our friendship was full of slumber parties and now somewhat embarrassing escapades.

As she sat back down in her seat, one last memory came to mind. This one, however, was not quite a happy one. Even though Andrea is only two weeks older than me, she is a grade ahead. I was born two days after the cut-off to be part of her class. When Andrea started her freshman year in high school, we drifted apart. She made new friends, and we both got involved in our own activities and interests. Even though it bothered me a great deal, I kept it to myself. She didn't seem heartbroken, so I acted like I wasn't either.

For two-and-a-half long years we went about our lives separately. Our friendship dwindled to a nod in the hallway at school or maybe a "hello" on rare occasions. I wanted to talk to her so badly. I would go to the phone to call her, but would hang up before the call went through. I was afraid that she wouldn't want to talk to me. The truth was, she wanted to call me, too, but would hang up for the exact same reason. We found out later that even though the other hadn't known it, we were both hurting and longing for the friendship we used to have.

I don't even know how it happened. I guess we finally realized that we had had too good of a friendship to ignore each other any longer. The months ahead held a lot of catching up. We found out that we were experiencing many of the same things and that we understood each other like no one else. We began what we later called cocoa talks. Even when the weather was warm, we would spend the evening sitting on Andrea's front steps, drinking hot cocoa with marshmallows and talking about everything that was going on in our lives. We laughed, and we cried. Sometimes we laughed so hard it made us cry. No matter what, we always left feeling better, feeling understood. It's been a bumpy road, but I wouldn't change any of it. In the nine years that she has lived across the street from me, we have formed an unbreakable bond of friendship that we both know is hard to come by. We are always asking each other how we got to be so lucky as to have our best friend living right across the street.

This next year holds uncertainty for both of us. Andrea will be starting college in the fall, and I will be left to survive my senior year alone. But one thing remains certain: Andrea and I have a friendship that will never graduate.

Laura Loken

My Brilliant Friend

My dearest friend, you've left me,
Standing all alone.
My body's numb with sorrow,
I don't know my way home.

I'm lost, depressed and frightened,
For you're not here with me.
And somewhere deep inside my heart,
My friend, you'll always be.

I know you couldn't help it,
And you didn't want to go,
But nonetheless you left me,
Sad and all alone.

Although I have my parents,
And other friends so close,
I don't know why it is,
But I love you, friend, the most.

Your kindness unto others,
Has washed up onto me,
You helped me out when times were tough,
And you helped to make me see.

You have been so good to me,
And as I let you go,
I know you were a true friend,
And for that I love you so.

For as long as I can recognize,
You've helped me to be strong,
And given me the courage and faith,
To keep on moving on.

So with my sad and heavy heart,
This part comes to an end.
But I will not say good-bye,
You'll always be my friend.

Benedicta Goveia

I Know Exactly What You Mean

Friendship is the hardest thing in the world to explain. It's not something you learn in school. But if you haven't learned the meaning of friendship, you really haven't learned anything.

Muhammad Ali

I was waiting anxiously by the phone when it rang, but still it startled me and I jumped. For a moment I was suddenly unable to move, and I stared at the phone as it rang again. Out of the corner of my eye I saw my little sister enter the room and stop to gawk at me. I guessed that I must have looked like an idiot, standing there staring at the phone as if I didn't know what to do with it when it made noise. As it rang again I broke from my trance and quickly snatched the receiver up from the cradle.

"Hello?"

"Hi," a shaking, choked voice said. "It's me." I wasn't used to hearing Annie's voice, but now it sounded as familiar as it had a couple of years ago.

Annie and I had been friends since we were little. All through elementary school we were the pair that everyone knew. Where one of us went, the other was sure to be right behind. But as we entered junior high, things began to change. Mainly, Annie began to change. Her social life became the most important thing to her, and being popular was what she strived for. She broke off from our circle of friends and joined a different, more popular crowd. I saw less and less of her, and when I did see her I felt uncomfortable and awkward, like we were strangers. Whether she tried to or not, Annie made me feel like I was inferior to her, not cool enough to hang around her, which hurt like nothing else I had known before.

I knew she didn't feel that way; she told me often how good a friend I was. And I knew she was going through a lot of confusion about herself, trying to find where she fit into the scheme of junior high. So I gave her some leeway and let her do some soul searching. Even though we were not as tight as we were when we were younger, we were still friends, even if I cared more about the relationship than she did at times. Often, though, I wished for the closeness, the sisterhood we had a couple of years ago. Things had been so simple then. They were easily defined: Annie and I were best friends, and we could talk to each other about anything. Now, everything was complicated. I was closer to other friends than I was to Annie, and there were things I told them that I never would tell her. It just wasn't like it was when we were younger, and I wondered if we would even be able to achieve the kind of relationship we had before things started changing.

"Hi," I said again, unable to think of any other reply. It had been so long since I had actually talked to Annie, not counting the brief moment before school today when she told me with worry in her eyes, "I think he's going to dump me."

I hadn't had time to answer her then, or when she came to me during lunch and said, "I have to call you today."

The buzz going around school was that Annie and her boyfriend Cory were having problems, and at first I didn't believe it. They had been together for almost eight months, and even at the last dance a couple of weeks ago I had seen them sneaking a kiss between songs. But then when she had said to me early that morning, her face taut with nervousness and sadness, that she was afraid Cory was going to break up with her, I knew that everything going around school was probably true.

I pulled myself from my thoughts as the silence grew longer, and I was trying to think of something intelligent to say when I realized that there was not silence from the end of the line but muffled sobs.

"Oh, God," I sighed, and I felt so horrible for not noticing at first that she was in pain. "How are you doing?"

"Not good, not good at all," Annie managed to reply, her voice thick with tears. "Cory just broke up with me."

I couldn't speak for a minute. I knew that it was coming, deep inside my subconscious had told me that it was inevitable, but it just seemed like Annie and Cory would somehow survive anything. They had been together so long, it was hard to imagine them apart.

Finally, my voice returned to me. "Oh Annie, I'm so sorry," I breathed, hoping my words sounded as sincere as they were meant to be. I didn't know what else to say, so I just kept repeating my apology.

"I know, I know," Annie mumbled, and I heard her blow her nose.

"You must be so upset. I know how much you liked him."

"No, I didn't like him," Annie coughed, and I was confused until she added in a low and unwavering voice, "I loved him."

I was overwhelmed into silence. Annie had spoken those last three words with such honesty and intensity that it had thrown me into shocked silence. I hadn't known she had such strong feelings for Cory. I knew that they went to the movies and talked on the phone and stuff like that, but I had never known just how much Cory had meant to Annie. She had really cared about him with a love that I had yet to truly experience myself. It made me sad to realize that the only time Annie had really talked to me about her relationship was to tell me it was over.

"I never knew you felt that way about him," I admitted. "I mean, I knew you liked him, but I never knew you *loved* him."

"I did," Annie cried, and I heard her wipe her nose. "I really did."

"So, why'd he break up with you?" I asked, hoping I wasn't treading on unstable ground. "Did he give you a reason?"

Now Annie's tone held more contempt than sorrow. "Well, he said, 'I'm getting bored. I need some variety in my life.' Can you believe him? He just got sick of me," she wailed, her voice her own again, and full of anguish. "What did I do wrong?"

"You didn't do anything," I made sure to tell her quickly and firmly. "It wasn't your fault. *He's* the one who broke up with you. It's his problem. This breakup doesn't mean that there's something wrong with you. You're perfectly lovable just the way you are." I was full of words of wisdom, and I hadn't been able to share that with Annie in a while.

"I guess you're right," Annie murmured, but I could tell she wasn't totally convinced. There was nothing I could do about that. I couldn't change how she felt about herself; all I could do was make sure to be there for her when she needed some encouraging words.

Through the phone I could hear Annie starting to cry again, and the sound made me hurt inside. It reminded me of the time when another boy Annie had liked dumped her, and I remember hugging her as she cried on my window seat. I had told her then that she would get through it, and she had, which meant that she could get over this, too. When I spoke, I made sure to keep my voice gentle and calm. "You two had such a long, wonderful time together, though, right?"

I thought maybe I detected a hint of a smile in Annie's voice when she replied. "Oh, yeah, definitely. The best."

"I never heard a lot about the relationship," I pointed out. "Tell me about it."

And suddenly she was talking to me. Serious, just-like-old-times talking. Remembering brought painful memories up to the surface, but also pleasant ones, and she started to laugh more often than she cried. As we talked, I could almost feel the gap of two years starting to close, and even though I knew it wouldn't stay closed long, I was just happy that we could regain our old friendship, even just for a little bit. Things felt back to normal again, almost perfect. But even though I tried to tell myself otherwise, I knew this wouldn't last. The next time Annie and a guy break up, we will have this conversation again, and things will feel normal. Yet, in between the start of a new relationship and the end of it, I will be second to Annie's new boyfriend, her new friends, her new clothes, her new schedule, her new personality. We will revert back to what we had been only last week—acquaintances. Distant friends.

I didn't care. I had other friends, other activities, other ideas to explore. Our lives would continue on separately, mine going one way, hers the other. I understood that. We were two different people now, with different views, attitudes, personalities, lives. We weren't as close as before, but we were still friends, and I wasn't the kind of person to drop old friends for new. Maybe Annie didn't care as much about our friendship as I did, maybe sometimes I was there for her more than she was there for me, and maybe sometimes I came second on Annie's list. I knew this, and I didn't care. I would always be there for Annie. We had been friends for so long, and I wasn't about to give that up.

"I have to go soon. I promised Bailey I'd call her tonight. But first, I want to thank you," Annie said, and her voice, I knew, was sincere. "You've always been such a good friend, Melinda. I know I must bore you to death with all this, but you still listen. Thanks." Annie knew what a good friend was; she just couldn't find it in herself to apply the knowledge. She was too confused, too unsure of herself, too caught up in the rush of teenage life. I understood that, too.

"I'm glad you're feeling better," I said sincerely. The conversation was coming to a close.

Annie thought for a minute. "It's going to take a long time to heal. I'm just going to miss him for a while." Annie grew more reflective, and her voice softer, more thoughtful, as she struggled to put her feelings into words. "We were so close. . . . It almost feels . . . It almost feels like a part of me has been taken away, a part I can't get back." She struggled for words. "Like . . . things feel different, like they won't ever be the same again." Annie sighed, frustrated. "Do you get what I'm trying to say?"

My voice was wobbly, and my cheeks were wet. "I know exactly what you mean," I told her. And I did understand—every word she said.

Melinda Favreau

For Better or For Worse®
by Lynn Johnston

Drowning

I look at you and my anger rages like an ocean,
A vast sea of wasted feelings,
And precious time.

Hurt by the things you say and do to me,
And the things you don't think I hear,
Or you don't think I'll find out.

They always find their way back to me.
And the gaps and oceans
Between us grow wider and vaster and deeper.

As words get between us until
Neither of us know what to say,
And nothing is left to do but turn around,
And look the other way.

Telling lies
To let the other one know who's not hurt the most
When really all it does is tear me up inside.

My empty heart is screaming
Fighting against the currents
Of love and hate, pulling away from each other,
Like the moon and the ocean
As we grow farther apart.

I want to talk,
To try to work things out and
Repair the rift that keeps growing.
But words get in the way.
We get angrier and more frustrated.

But how do I explain
How I feel and how much I want
To whisper between classes,
And go on double dates,
And share clothes and eat ice cream and giggle.
Spend the night making fish faces until we laugh so hard
    our sides split,
And do all the things that used to be important,
But are now forbidden
Because one of us might let our guard down
And say or do something that will make the other angry.

When truthfully things like dancing to Hootie and the
    Blowfish,
Tripping up stairs and strange Polaroid pictures
Are things only a best friend can understand.

But somehow as I sit here and write this,
Not because I want to but because I have to for you and
    for myself,
The rift seems to heal itself and the ocean doesn't seem
    quite so bottomless.

And I'm smiling again.
Because I know you will read this,
And understand it and me, and the way I feel.

Because you always have and I know you always will.
It's that bond that reaches over oceans and repairs torn
    hearts,
Something that only a best friend can understand.

Rebecca Slobada

Two Girls and a Friendship

The weak can never forgive. Forgiveness is the attribute of the strong.

Mahatma Gandhi

Among the trinkets and decorative items in a fifteen-year-old girl's room, one stood out boldly—a bright blue clay vase with colorful painted flowers. Not a perfect or beautiful vase, this one is broken in several places. The owner of the vase has carefully mended it, but spiderlike cracks remain. If this vase could talk, it would tell the story of two girls and a friendship.

Amy and June met on an airplane on their way home from Bangkok where their fathers, who were business partners, were attending meetings. June sat behind Amy. Halfway toward home, Amy turned around hesitantly and gave June a bright blue vase made of clay. It was a small gesture, but a token of friendship and an introduction. June accepted, and they smiled shyly at each other. And on that day, a simple friendship between two four-year-olds was established.

Years flew by. Amy and June grew up together, played

together, studied together and, naturally, became each other's closest confidante. June cried on Amy's shoulder when her little puppy died in a car accident. June was there for Amy when she fell during a gymnastic routine in the talent show and everyone had laughed at her. When June ran away at the age of ten after an argument with her mother, it was Amy who convinced her to go back home. And it was June who comforted Amy when Amy's favorite uncle passed away. June was part of Amy, as Amy was part of June.

Life is not, and never will be, a bed of roses. People change as they grow up, for better or for worse. Sometimes these changes are hard to accept. And even the most special friendships can be destroyed. When she was fourteen, Amy met a boy. A boy, to fourteen-year-old Amy, was heaven-sent. Amy started hanging out with this boy all the time, and she started to see less and less of June. And although June was hurt, she tried to be understanding. She was still there for Amy when Amy had arguments with her boyfriend and needed a shoulder to cry on. But Amy wasn't there when June needed her. June was going through a difficult period and found herself mildly depressed. But Amy still leaned on June for relationship support. Upset and depressed about the state of their friendship, June invited Amy to her house to talk. When June tried to bring up her difficulties and her problems, Amy brushed her off by saying, "Later." Instead, Amy asked June for ideas for what she should buy for her boyfriend on their half-year anniversary. June couldn't take it anymore. Anger, sadness, resentment, betrayal and disappointment washed over her. June exploded. She started crying and yelling at Amy.

"What am I to you, Amy? Your friend or just your little dog?" June cried. June was hoping for an apology and some support. Instead, Amy was defensive and yelled back at June. A friendship of ten years was disintegrating before their eyes. And there was nothing either of them could do about it.

"That's it, June! I hate you!" Amy yelled. There was no way of taking it back. June stared at Amy tearfully. Amy broke eye contact and spun around on her heel and stomped out of June's room, slamming the door hard behind her. A blue vase on the shelf jumped and fell onto the floor, smashing into several pieces. Unstoppable tears flowed freely as June knelt down on the floor and picked up the pieces. No more giggling, no more gossiping, no more endless sleepovers and no more long phone sessions with her best friend. Ten years of friendship . . . shattered like the vase, the vase that she had so preciously taken care of all these years, the vase that symbolized all that was wonderful about friendship.

The pain of losing a best friend, losing the one you trusted most, is worse than a thousand stabbing knives. Collapsing into a heap on the floor, June cried uncontrollably. This was not one of the stupid arguments she and Amy had sometimes. This was serious and possibly irreparable. A horrible emptiness filled her heart. She knew they had lost that special bond between them. She also knew there was no way of bringing it back. It was over.

At school, June and Amy were stiff and polite with one another. Not long after their argument, Amy broke up with her boyfriend. But both were stubborn, and remained icy and distant. Amy had not forgiven June for June's cruel words. And even June could not find a place in her heart where she could forgive Amy. Hurt and betrayal took time to heal. Sort of like the vase. The broken pieces lay unmended in June's dresser drawer. Even if it was put back together again, no matter how carefully, cracks would remain. A broken vase could never be perfect again.

One year passed. It was June's fifteenth birthday. Instead of feeling happy, June only felt gloom. She remembered her fourteenth birthday, one month before their big fight. It had been a great one, and they had been so happy. They had giggled over the silliest things and engaged in a food fight. They had vowed their friendship would last for an eternity. Bittersweet tears filled June's eyes. She could still remember an image of four-year-old Amy holding out the blue vase to her.

The doorbell rang. June hopped up and rushed to the door. She was expecting her cousin. The door swung open. June froze. Amy stood at the doorstep, holding a small package. "I just wanted to say, well, I . . ." The former best friends looked at each other, their emotions mirrored on each other's faces. "Hap . . . happy birthday, June," Amy finally stammered out. She shoved the gift into June's hand and ran down the pathway. June felt compelled to chase after her, but she didn't. Instead, she closed the door gently.

Going to her room, she sat down on her bed and opened the gift. It was a bracelet. Attached to it was a note that read, "Dear June, Happy Fifteenth Birthday, Amy." At the bottom was a small, "P. S. I'm sorry." Two words. Two simple words that filled June's heart with joy. She picked up the phone to call Amy. And made a mental note to mend her broken vase. Even though it would never be perfect, an imperfect vase was better than a shattered one.

Pey Jung Yeong

For Better or For Worse®
by Lynn Johnston

FOR BETTER OR FOR WORSE ©*United Features Syndicate. Reprinted by Permission.*

For Such a Time as This

We all need each other.

Leo Buscaglia

My friend is so beautiful but she is blind to it. She has exotic dark features with full lips and flashing eyes. Her figure is one that many girls would kill to have, and her sense of style is undeniable. Although her beauty is so evident on the outside, it's what she has inside, her heart, that draws so many people to her. Her kindness and compassion, her spirituality, and especially her sense of humor. She can make me crack up with a certain face or a noise. And this girl's voice is that of an angel. Talented in innumerable ways, she plays sports, dances and is an honor student. From group to group she flits, a social butterfly, unaware of the cliques, thinking each group is a different type of exquisite flower, each having different, but equally delicious nectar. Her many friends are constantly vying for her attention and approval, advice and comfort. She is popular, not through fear, but by friendliness and authenticity. Which is why I can't understand how this wonder of a woman can possibly feel the way she does: worthless.

Not many know the self-loathing she feels. I am one of the few who have been granted a tiny peek into her mixed-up world. I say mixed-up because my friend just can't see her loveliness and realize her value. Stress runs her life, and anxiety is her constant companion. Pressure, she feels, is unavoidable. She wants it all to end, her pain to be banished forever, but she covers these unfathomable contemplations with extra smiles and laughter. There is no laughter when she is all alone and her mind is telling her she's nothing; the smiles are replaced with blank stares, and the sense of nothingness returns.

What does one do when they see their friend like this, a shell of what they once were? How does one convince this miracle of the beauty she possesses, and that she is loved by others, when she can't love herself, and not even be able to look herself in the eye? This girl doesn't know how much she means to me: countless times lifting me up, cheering me on, listening to my sobs and crying with me. If this girl is taken away from me, I will be dead inside, for we are joined by something greater than us. Nothing can replace what we have, and I will stand by her side always, lifting her up, cheering her on, listening to her sobs and crying with her. I will repay her for what she has done for me, and I will strive to keep her alive. I have been placed in her life for such a time as this.

Sarah Klapak

Sorrows Underneath

I think of all my problems.
I think of all my pain.
I think of all my sorrows,
Until I go insane.

I think of all the smiles I've worn,
Which hide sorrows underneath.
No one seems to notice,
That I go through so much grief.

My tears seem to keep flowing,
Inside my tired eyes.
Each time I want to tell you,
My words come out as lies.

These days I'm feeling distant,
Far away and weak.
My sadness pulls me further,
From the happiness I seek.

I've just begun to realize,
That my hopes and dreams are gone,
I'm walking down a dead-end road,
Humming a tuneless song.

I'm standing on a rooftop,
Although I'm scared of heights,
I'm watching the cars beneath me move,
And somehow this doesn't feel right.

Now I think of what I'm doing,
I know I should find a way,
To beat through my depression,
Will I be able to someday?

Someone might be there,
To help me make it through,
Maybe they will listen,
And tell me what to do.

I'm seeing through the darkness,
And I'm starting to trust a few,
I think I'll try to make it,
So I can be there for them, too.

Zihanna Rahman

The Sisters I Never Had

When I was in junior-high school, the singer Sinead O'Connor released an album called "I Do Not Want What I Haven't Got." If that's true, she's the only person who doesn't. Everyone longs for what they lack. The overweight imagine how perfect their lives would be if they could just lose whatever number of pounds. The bone-thin fantasize about how they would look if they could only grow breasts. The short want to be tall. The tall want to shrink out of sight. The single want a mate. The attached want independence. And, of course, all only children want a sibling.

Except me.

The only child of two wonderfully supportive, happily married parents, I drank in the attention. I got all the hugs and all the kisses. At holidays and birthdays, every dime went to my presents. When I needed my father's help with math, I didn't have to wait in line behind a crew of other perplexed kids.

I was first. I was only. And, being a fairly bright girl, I knew a good thing when I saw it. Why would I want some other kid to screw it up?

All my girlfriends with sisters were always complaining

about some misdeed their sib had done—ignoring them, tagging along too much, borrowing clothes without asking, etc., etc.

Who needs it? I thought. *I never want to have a sister.*

Or so I thought. Ever the spoiled only child, I went to a private high school, an all-girls school. I know it makes a lot of people cringe, but to me, it was paradise. I had been an outcast in junior high, but here I found several girls to whom I related in ways I never thought possible. They didn't roll their eyes when I said something stupid. They forgave me when I lost my temper. They didn't think I was a loser because I liked school too much. They were more than friends. They were family. I truly felt they were the sisters I never had. And the school encouraged this view.

Every freshman was matched with a senior who would be her "big sister." Your big sister's friends, if they liked you, called themselves your "surrogate" big sister. Their little sisters then became your sisters by connection. Before I knew it, I went from being an only child to the member of a huge family, adopting sisters left and right.

Around that time, my friend Marjke (my friend since age five, and still my best), with whom I had been feuding for a few years, became my buddy again. She has a sister and two brothers and, as will happen, wasn't really thrilled with them all the time. She would tell me all her problems with school, her family and anything else that was bothering her. Then she would turn to me and say, "You're like the big sister I never had." Every time she said it, I was flattered. I loved the idea of being so close to someone that they considered you family. I still love it. Marjke is still like my sister. And her sister, Gretchen, also is like my sister. And my friends from high school that I keep in touch with are like my sisters.

After all those years of childhood denying I wanted

siblings, I went out and selected my own. And no, I don't always get along with them. We fight. We lose touch from time to time. We disappoint each other.

But always, at some core level, we share a connection with each other. We know how to make each other laugh, how to comfort each other in times of sadness. We know how to be there for each other. That is, after all, what sisterhood is all about.

Amanda Cuda

Love Letter to the Card Corner

Do not go where the path may lead; go instead where there is no path and leave a trail.

Ralph Waldo Emerson

We called it the Card Corner. It was a place for the sub-versive girls—girls who the other girls at our school thought odd, not popular enough, not trendy enough. Girls who listened to music the other girls didn't like. It was a place for girls who didn't fit in, who'd been dumped by their friends for being too weird—as I had been.

Before we took it over, there was nothing remarkable about the Card Corner. It was a brown-carpeted nook on the first floor of the old classroom building. There was a dilapidated brown cabinet there, a leaky radiator and a door that led outside to the green lawns where girls some-times ate lunch. It was nothing much to look at—but to me it was a haven, a place of magic and rebellion, of friend-ship and hilarity and schemes for the future.

We started calling it the Card Corner because at first some of us played card games there. I never did, not once, and after awhile, no one else did either—we were too busy talking—but the name stuck. The old brown cabinet was empty before we started using it. I suppose it was for decorative purposes.

I don't remember which of us first kept her schoolbooks in the cabinet instead of using a locker, but pretty soon most of us did. It just happened that way, just as we had gravitated towards each other, though we weren't all in the same grade.

Maybe Debby was the catalyst. At sixteen, she was a terrific visual artist, knew lots about music, had gone to lots of rock shows, and her boyfriend was the lead singer of a rock band. She was beautiful but thought herself fat.

My whole world opened up when Debby took me to my first nightclub show a month before my fifteenth birthday. Her boyfriend's band played, and I got a crush on her boyfriend's brother Jonathan, who was also in the band. Many of the Card Corner girls went to that show, and afterwards we all spent the night at Debby's. Everything seemed different to me after that night— brighter, more exciting. After that, I began to spend all my time with Debby and the other girls—Sylvia, Josie, Hillary. At any point there might have been seven or ten or twelve of us hanging out together at school, going to nightclubs, going shopping for music or clothes.

Some Card Corner girls were outwardly rebellious— like Debby, who wore a leather jacket with her uniform gray skirt and white blouse. Some were more quiet and intellectual, but felt at home in the Corner, where they could be themselves, unfashionable though that might be. I wrote stories and music reviews for the school paper. Debby drew pictures of all of us and amazing cartoons chronicling our weekend adventures. Josie was on the swim team, and Joan was a gymnast. I couldn't do gymnastics to save my life, but among the Card Corner contingent, that didn't seem to matter.

When we got to school in the morning, we'd congregate at the Corner. Sometimes one or two of us would sit on top of the cabinet, while others would sit on the carpet and on the step that led to the door. If it were a cold day, we might huddle by the radiator if it was working. Debby would pull out her notebook with the black-and-white marbled cover, and if I were lucky, she would sketch a portrait of Jonathan. At lunch or free period we'd meet at the Corner. It's not that we didn't hang out at other spots at school, in the lunchroom or out on the terrace with the round green tables. But this was our spot, ours alone.

The school administration wasn't thrilled that we'd taken over the brown cabinet, but they didn't do anything about it—not yet. They weren't thrilled with us in general, for we showed a remarkable lack of "school spirit." Instead we backed each other up, were strong together. I finally had friends with whom I belonged. Sylvia told me that her former friends, who'd dropped her a while before, walked past her one day and commented to each other, "She has such weird friends now!" We thought that hilarious and somewhat of a compliment.

We would talk about how we'd been dropped by our previous cliques, and how we'd found each other. Once Josie and I talked with my mom about this, and she didn't seem to get how lucky we felt. She seemed to think we still felt bad about being dumped. She didn't realize that we knew we'd found the real thing, real friendship. We knew how different it was from what we'd had before.

By the time I became a junior, a number of my friends had graduated, and there weren't so many Card Corner girls left at the school. A week or two into fall semester, we walked into the Corner and found all our books piled in a heap on the carpet, the cabinet gone. The administration had finally done something about us. We had to start using lockers again, though we still gathered together at the Card Corner. It wasn't the same, with so many of my friends no longer there—but they remained my friends, nonetheless. And I had gained something: a sense of who I was, a sense of what it was to love and be loved by true friends.

Gwynne Garfinkle

Nerds

It's not cool to be a nerd. You get teased a lot. You get picked last in gym class. You don't get invited to the cool parties. I realize that Bill Gates has committed the ultimate revenge of the nerds by taking over the world, but even having a multi-billionaire poster boy to represent us doesn't really help when you're not part of the cool scene.

But at least I'm not alone. I have my friend Dave. You can probably survive almost any experience—however humiliating or degrading—if you have someone to share it with. Junior high for Dave and I was like spending a few years in a foxhole together. There was constant combat, we always had to be on the defensive, and we never knew when the "cool" people might strike.

Dave and I met in seventh grade on the nerd mobile, the school bus. We live near each other, which is far from school. This afforded us a lot of time to try to plot our own "revenge." Of course, we never have carried out any of our elaborate, nonviolent schemes. But it's fun to imagine the looks on everyone's faces when they report for roll call at gym only to find their gym shoes Krazy-glued in place, or for everyone to show up at the gym for the big pep rally only to find the doors Krazy-glued shut. For some reason our schemes always seem to involve Krazy glue—don't ask me why.

Dave's a bit louder than me. I tend toward the quiet side. We both share a love of conspiracy theories. We've both seen every episode of *The X-Files*. Dave's a little more into it than I am. He sort of believes everything has some hidden meaning. Not in a freaky weird way—well, I guess maybe a little freaky—but not enough to scare anyone. Dave's a little bigger than me. We're sort of a Laurel and Hardy pair—I'm the skinny nerd and Dave's the chubby one. You've seen us. Every school has a set. I'm always trying to get Dave to eat a little less, and he's always trying to get me to eat a little more. But most importantly, we share the ultimate common bond—neither one of us is cool. I don't know exactly what it is that separates the "cool" from the "nerd." Okay, so I'm not so great at sports and I always get A's in English. Is that a crime?

We spend about half our time wishing we could be cool and the other half making fun of the cool people. It just seems better somehow to be one of them instead of one of us. I've heard all the stuff about how having to work harder for something builds character. And I've seen all the movies where the nerdy guy gets the girl in the end because the cool guy turns out to be a big jerk. But that's not how it seems to work out in real life. Dave and I like to talk about our fantasies—like what if there was some sort of natural disaster, like lightning struck the school and everyone was trapped, and only we could figure out how to save everyone because we were smarter than they were. And then they would be so grateful to us that we would inherit the cool throne. Those opportunities don't come up too often. It's kind of like pretending what it would be like if you won the lottery and thinking about all the cool things you could buy.

Well, one day we sort of did win the lottery. Dave and I

are both into comedy, so we're always acting out scenes from our favorite shows. Most of the time, people think we're nuts, but they pretty much think that anyway, so we might as well have fun. We were at lunch doing a scene from our all-time favorite movie, *American Pie*: after Jim's dad catches him, you know, with the pie. We were totally cracking each other up. I was Jim, and Dave played Jim's dad. It just sort of spontaneously happened. Dave and I were talking about the movie, and all of a sudden we were doing the scene and reciting the lines.

We were eating our lunch in this big outdoor area we call the "graveyard" because it has these big rocks you can sit on that sort of look like gravestones. It sounds a little creepy, but when everyone calls it that and you go there every day, it sort of stops being creepy. Anyway, we were totally into it and didn't notice anyone else was around.

I was acting embarrassed and Dave, as Jim's dad, was acting, well, like Jim's dad. Acting embarrassed kind of comes easy to me, so I guess it was method acting on my part. We got to the end of the scene and suddenly there was a round of applause. We both looked up, and it was all girls. And not just any girls—Heather and Megan and Courtney—the cool girls. Our first reaction was, of course, that they were mocking us.

But somehow the Earth must have begun spinning backward on its axis or the gravitational pull of the sun had suddenly stopped because we were being acknowledged, and not in the form of having our lockers TP'd or getting a Melvin. They were genuinely laughing. Heather said, "You guys are great. How do you remember all that stuff?" And Megan chimed in with, "That's so cool; it's like watching the movie." We just stood there with our mouths open. There was nothing left to do but start the band-camp scene. I played Jim again, and Dave put aside his self-pride and took on the role of the band-camp girl.

We still had the rhythm, and the girls didn't leave. They kept laughing. "Do the scene where Stiffler's mom comes in," one of them squealed.

Although our moment in the sun seemed to go on for hours, it was interrupted about two seconds later when Heather's and Megan's and Courtney's boyfriends showed up. "What is this, a dweebathon?" they asked. The six of them left, but not before the girls turned back and smiled at us. Dave and I had a moment.

I don't think anything's changed as a result. Of course, Dave and I have memorized all the dialogue from both *American Pie* movies now. "Band camp from *Pie 2*, you say?" We take our little show on the road every day at lunch, but it's hard to recreate the magic. We just keep hoping. We still have to ride the bus to school every day. We still get picked last and second-to-last for softball, touch football, volleyball, soccer, field hockey, basketball, foosball . . . you get the idea. I'm still getting an A in English.

Yet something is different. We had a moment of glory. We were out there, exposed for all the world to see, and the world recognized us. Well, not exactly the world, but CHEERLEADERS!

We don't have to wonder anymore what it is like to be cool. Okay, five minutes of being cool does not a cool person make. We'd still like to be cool all the time. But having that moment, and having it together, was this great experience that we shared. We don't have to spend our time wondering, and we both know what we are capable of. That should at least get us through sophomore year.

Owen Rosen

My Friend and I Are Different

My friend is a man with three grandchildren.
Two generations separate us.
He tells me stories about his youth
And I listen.

My friend is a lesbian and she smiles into the sun.
We both see beauty in others but in different ways.
Sometimes she cries, but so do I.
Usually we laugh together and drink coffee.

My friend cannot speak English.
He is from a world far away
Where he learned to paint with berries
And play instruments made of animal skin.
We were born on the same day,
And ask each other questions with our hands.

My friend is a Catholic.
We talk about the one God we all share,
Every religion dancing under the same sun,
Same God.

I tell her that I am Jewish because of my father,
And Christian because of my mother.
I tell her that I feel proud,
And am glad.

My friend lives in darkness, for she is blind.
She can see with her ears and her nose.
She can sense when I am sad,
She can smell my tears in the air.
I tell her how beautiful she is and she nods, taking my face
   in her hand.
"And you are beautiful, too."

My friend is homeless.
He lives on the beach and plays the guitar.
I ask him questions and he answers me.
He doesn't ask for money,
He just wants to hear game scores.
Every day he tells me to follow my dreams.

My friend is three feet tall.
She asks me if she is normal.
"No," I say. "Wouldn't that be sad?"
She nods and laughs.
"It would be sad," she says,
". . . to be normal."

My friend looks just like me.
She has green eyes and blonde hair
And we have the same ideas and experiences.
And when I turn my back to the mirror,
Everyone looks a little bit different.

Zoe Graye

Unsinkable Friendship

"Delicia, Sarah is supposed to be coming over, so would you mind if she went with us?" Jen asked me over the phone.

"Sarah . . . Wagonlit?"

"Yeah."

"Well, um . . . I guess."

"You sure?"

"Uh huh." *Right. Sarah. Snob.*

"K. We'll be over about five-thirty."

"Okay. Bye."

Great. Sarah was coming to see *Titanic* with us. Sarah WAGONLIT.

She'll probably ignore me all night.

I never really liked her. She was one of *them.* Her and her long, shiny hair, bright blue eyes, perfect skin and flawless makeup. With trendy clothes and several boyfriends under her belt, she was popular, unlike me. Delicia. I didn't have boyfriends. I had boy *friends.* I wasn't beautiful like her. I didn't even want to count how many guys liked her, or I might become ill. Not that I didn't have friends. I did, I just wasn't ever one of them: the cool ones. The ones with the great hair, the great clothes, the great everything. I was always just Delicia to them. That one girl in drama class.

So why would I be going to see *Titanic* with an obvious member of "them"? Well, she's a friend of Jen's. They are both on the softball team. That's why.

Five-thirty rolls around and Jen and Sarah pull up. "Hey, Delicia."

Omigosh, she's in my house. Does my house smell weird? NO! Mom's making that Salisbury steak again; doesn't she know it smells funky? Great, Sarah probably thinks we eat road kill. Just great.

"Let's go, girls." My mom ushers us out the door and into the car. The whole ride to the mall I talk to Jen, and occasionally make eye contact with Sarah. Hey, I'm making progress here. Finally, we get to the mall and go inside the theater. Despite the fact that this is my fifth time seeing *Titanic*, I cry anyway. I hear sniffles coming from Jen and Sarah, too.

All that week at school I kept seeing Sarah in between classes. She would smile at me as we passed each other in the hall. Sometimes she would even say hi.

The next Saturday I was sitting at home when the phone rang.

"Hello?"

"Delicia? This is Sarah."

"Oh, um. Hey, Sarah."

"Hi. Jen said to call you and see if you wanted to go see *Titanic* with us again."

"Uhh . . . well . . . sure."

"Okay, she said she'd pick us up around seven-thirty."

"Okay."

"Well, see you then."

"Bye."

Six-thirty came around and the phone rang again. "Hello?"

"Delicia . . . this is Sarah again. Jen can't go."

"Oh . . ."

"Her parents are making her go out to dinner with the whole family."

"Oh . . . well . . . that's okay. Maybe we could all go again sometime . . . so I'll talk to you later or something . . ."

"Wait . . . umm . . . I was thinking that maybe . . . you would . . . like to go with just me?" she asked.

Whoa. I wasn't prepared for that. Me go to a movie with Sarah? She wanted to spend time with just *me?*

"Yeah. Sure. I mean, of course," I stuttered. Wow.

"Okay, cool! I'll pick you up in . . . about fifteen minutes. . . . Is that okay?"

"Yeah, sure!"

"K, see ya then . . . bye."

Omigosh.

I ran upstairs to check my hair and my makeup. I looked fine, decent. Fifteen minutes later came a knock on the door. "Hey, ready to go?" Sarah asked.

"Yeah."

That night was the beginning of a long friendship. We connected in a way I would never have expected. She was completely different than how I had stereotyped her in my mind. All during that summer Sarah and I went to see that movie six or seven more times together. We started doing countless other things together, too. We became inseparable: sisters. I felt like I had known Sarah all my life.

That was years ago. Looking back on it, I can see that I was the snob. I had decided what kind of person Sarah was before I even got to know her. Now I know that people aren't what they seem. I was lucky enough to get to know her for who she really is, and I'm thankful that I did. She is a huge part of my life now—my very best friend. One thing's for sure: Not even the *Titanic* could sink our friendship.

Delicia Dudley

Friendship Is Like a Flower

Friendship is like a flower,
Glowing in its glory,
Each and every seed,
Telling its own story.

As each flower blooms,
And then continues to grow,
More of its strength and knowledge,
Continues to show.

And like a garden,
It blooms much more fair,
When carefully tended,
By those who care.

Once in a while,
You come across a friend,
Who is beautiful as a flower,
With a good heart to lend.

So I picked this flower,
And pulled it apart,
And soon all its pieces,
Grew into my heart.

But what I realized,
Is that this flower that grew,
Was not leaves and petals,
But pieces of you.

Your love and kindness,
Your strength and power,
Have helped me grow,
Into my own little flower.

And now with our friendship,
I'll never let go,
And we can help others,
To flower and grow.

Jenifer Sunday

Choosing a Broken Heart

Maturity begins to grow when you can sense your concern for others outweighing your concern for yourself.

John Macnaughton

"This is it," he told me, looking up at the fresh night sky. It was just minutes before the sun was about to shy away under a world which I had only known for eighteen years. My best friend, Christine, had been around for the last three of them. Nothing had ever threatened our friendship until we met Trey.

"I know," I whispered back, my eyes shut, my fingers lost in his chocolate curls as we lay on an abandoned soccer field. We didn't care about the plans we had made or whatever it was we had to do on that vulnerable summer night—we had a chance to escape, and we took it.

We laid in silence, my eyes still shut tight. Those milky-white stars must have looked so incredible floating in that black sea of night, but I couldn't open my eyes because if I set my tears loose, Trey might have felt as guilty as I did just then. Christine never knew we were together that night—or that I had fallen for him just as hard as she had from the moment he became our friend.

I felt Trey turn toward me. We weren't sure what we were doing, lying on that field, both of us knowing that my most wonderful friend ever was just miles away, her heart set on belonging to the irresistible Trey.

"Look at me, Kara." The warm, July breeze overtook my heart and gave it breath as he spoke to me. My pulse shivered and my bones turned to silk as I let his velvet brown eyes catch hold of the restless desire that was chained behind my green ones. "We haven't done anything wrong yet, you know," he said, kissing my forehead and then my nose. Half of me wanted to scream at him for being born while the other half just wanted him to kiss me and make me forget about everything that I would be throwing away. Just because Christine had wiped away my every tear and knew every one of my faults but still insisted on loving me until the end, didn't mean I couldn't fall in love with the same guy she was in love with, right? I had to make a choice. Who was I willing to lose?

"Maybe we should . . . keep it that way," I choked out. My heart shattered as I realized at that instant that I would never be able to kiss this amazing person who now belonged to a person just as amazing as him: Christine. But my heart was simply wrong this time, and I had to break it myself.

The entire night went by with us laughing, talking, crying and laughing a little more. When the sun started to hover over us and reveal the tear stains on my face, we both knew it was time to leave. Trey put his arm around me as we walked to our cars in a haze of piercing reality.

"So I guess these past several hours of quality time with you has upgraded me to a best friend now, huh?" Trey asked, scratching his head and grinning at me.

"Yeah . . . and since we're best friends now I guess it's

pretty safe for me to tell you your breath really stinks." I winked and smiled back at him as I got inside my car, taking one last look at that soccer field.

I could have driven away that morning in love with someone who had the most rare and powerful charisma I'd ever encountered, but instead I drove away gaining a new best friend, while still holding on to the most loyal and magnificent human being I ever met, my Christine.

Kara MacDonald

One Step Behind

Each day is an endless parade to a destination unknown,
Life leading you on an unmarked path not clearly shown.
Some parts of your path may be rugged and steep,
And others have crevasses infinitely deep.

There are times on your journey where to go, you know not,
For in a dense fog, your body is caught.
Unable to see what lies ahead of the way,
Uncertain to when this haze will eventually stray.

There are times when I am caught in this confusion, too,
Not knowing where to go, not knowing what to do.
But no matter how dense the fog when I turn I see,
Your smiling face looking back at me.

With reassurance in your glance,
I know you'll always be there,
Only one step behind,
each step taken with care.

I hope that you know, when you are lost in the mist,
Feeling unloved, alone and unmissed,
That if you glance back, you will find,
That I will be there, only one step behind.

Christy Vander Griendt

Forever Beyond a Good-Bye

I waited patiently until the mailman placed the mail into each of the mailboxes and drove away before I checked to see if my much-anticipated college acceptance letter had arrived. I truly believed that since my abusive father had finally moved out of the house a month before, and I was developing an unbreakable bond with my mother and brother, that things were finally on the right track and nothing could go wrong. I wasn't ready to handle any additional downers in my life.

I opened the mailbox with drops of water from an afternoon rain shower tracing through my hands. I searched anxiously through every envelope. My eyes finally landed on a small envelope with the name of my hopeful future college printed on its face. I vaguely remembered someone saying that the small envelopes only contained letters of rejection. I quickly muted that thought. As I opened the tiny envelope, all my fears were born into reality. And drops of water now traced my face, all leading up to my eyes.

I jumped into my truck, afraid to go home and see the disappointment written across my mom's face. I drove to my only place of comfort and support—my best friend Dave's house. My stomach was doing so many flips that I had to stop the truck several times to catch my breath and regroup. I finally arrived at Dave's house, trying my hardest to keep my composure. I spent the next few hours sobbing to Dave about my lost future. He said all the right things that a best friend could say.

I was so full of anger, shame and fear that I decided tonight was going to be my last night on Earth. I knew that if I were to wake up the next day, I would see a smile on my dad's face as if to celebrate my lack of success—the only kid in the family who couldn't get into college—a bum with no future. I could not stand that my past, consisting of anger and sadness, was catching up with me.

I decided that it was time to leave Dave's house. I got up to say my good-byes, forever, but before I could open my mouth he grabbed me and gave me a huge hug and told me that he loved me, in a brotherly kind of way. As I sat in my truck to leave, he cradled my head in his hands and gave me a kiss on the side of my head. I closed my door and left—my eyes so filled with tears that I could barely see. As I left his driveway I whispered, "Good-bye forever," hoping that maybe he heard me.

I walked into my room and saw my butterfly knife staring at me, screaming that it was the answer. I then got in my truck and drove to a place where I knew I would be alone. I opened the butterfly knife and rested it on my wrist, contemplating the amount of pain that I would encounter before my life would end. I tightened up my arm with a "no-turning-back" expression painted on my face. Just as I placed the edge of the knife on my wrist, my cell phone rang and interrupted my focus. I couldn't understand why anyone would be calling me this late. I answered it.

Dave's voice cracked through my cell phone. "I'm just calling to tell you that I love you. I don't know what I would ever do without you."

With tears once again welling up in my eyes, I said, "I love you, too."

I put the knife away, drove home and went to sleep. A few weeks later, the first time either of us spoke of that night, Dave told me that he had an urgent feeling that he should call me and tell me he loved me. He called it a gut feeling or an intuition. I broke down and told him what his gut feeling had done for me, and for the first time I saw my best friend with a tear in his eye and a smile on his face as he told me life would just be "life" unless we experienced it together.

I now have a steady job with a future in the culinary arts. I live on Maui with my other best friend, my brother. I can never fully thank Dave enough or understand what kind of miracles actually took place that night. Or what's going to happen now since we live so far apart. But I do know he will be my best friend forever.

Adam Cohen
Submitted by Mary Olsen Kelly

Why They Are Friends

Because . . . they smile.

Because . . . they understand just by looking into your eyes.

Because . . . they finish your sentences and know what you like.

Because . . . they know you better than you know yourself.

Because . . . with them you aren't afraid to be yourself.

Because . . . you can say something stupid or expose your deepest secrets to them.

Because . . . everything you do together becomes a memory.

Because . . . you don't need to do something special to have fun . . . fun just happens.

Because . . . you don't need to explain anything . . . they just know.

Because . . . they tell you the truth, no matter how much you'd rather not hear it.

Because . . . they would do anything for you and get you out of trouble.

Because . . . they make you laugh harder than anyone.

Because . . . they are not afraid to put themselves on the line for you.

Because . . . you can trust them.

Because . . . they believe in your dreams, no matter how silly they may seem.

Because . . . they dry your tears.

Because . . . you are good enough when you are with them.

Because . . . they love you for who you really are.

Kristy Glassen

4

TOUGH TIMES

We cannot tell what may happen to us in the strange medley of life. But we can decide what happens in us, how we take it, what we do with it—and that is what really counts in the end.

Joseph Fort Newton

Through the Eyes of a Teenager

Every day passes,
Reminding me of lessons to be learned.
Opportunities pass me by,
Showing me things to be earned.

I do not know life as an adult sees it,
Only as a child and teen.
I can only guess what life is meant to be,
Based on what I've seen.

Today I learned of love,
And the pain that it may bear.
You can never know a person's truth,
Behind the masks they wear.

I do not know the meaning of love,
Or why it is never true.
I'm unsure of so many things these days,
I know less than I thought I knew.

I find it's getting difficult,
To distinguish bad from good.
And although it sounds cliché,
I'm a child misunderstood.

I need to move on past the hurts,
Move to heaven from this hell.
I need to stand up to others,
And to myself as well.

I don't know how to tell,
A good friend from a bad.
We talk behind each other's backs,
Ruining the trust we had.

When I stare into the mirror,
I see things I wish I could deny.
A fear of judgment and confrontation,
I can no longer look myself in the eye.

If everybody has to go,
Through torment and through pain.
If they understand the hurt,
That is another's gain.

If they can feel,
The burden of their fears.
And know the cost,
Of showing their tears.

If they know how it feels,
To have a lover or friend.
Stab their backs with knives,
Why are they so cruel to say
These are the best years of our lives?

Marissa Roche

Operation Save the World

But you be strong and do not lose courage, for there is reward for your work.

Chronicles 15:7

I always thought "it could never happen to me." To tell you the truth, I don't think the thought ever crossed my mind. I lived an extremely sheltered life living in a small town, and attended an all-girls Catholic high school. It all began the beginning of my sophomore year. It was right around homecoming, when I knew I had met the "man of my dreams," or so I thought. Carl was a living dream with a great personality, who always knew exactly what to say to make me feel like I was queen of the world. He seemed to have it all: star of the football team, captain of the wrestling team and president of his homeroom. He was so perfect and to think that he liked me was incredible! He wanted to spend every waking moment with me. I was a busy girl and a very good student. I was an athlete on the basketball and volleyball teams, student council class secretary, choreographer of my swing choir, and this year I was even elected to homecoming court. My life was picture-perfect.

The more time we spent together, the more he wanted me all to himself. I didn't object because I thoroughly enjoyed the time I spent with him. But then it began. It started with swearing and verbal arguments, but quickly escalated from there. I always thought I would never put up with that, but I soon realized there was nothing that I could do. I discovered that Carl had problems.

He confided in me, and I found out all about his divorced parents and abusive father. I felt it was my duty to take care of him because he wasn't as fortunate as I to have two loving parents who gave me the world. Little did I realize, I was sacrificing myself for his punishing behavior. I was also sacrificing the friendships of my three best friends. I was becoming extremely isolated and growing farther and farther apart from my family and younger sister. Carl now took up all of my time, and I considered it my responsibility to rescue him. I'm not the type of person who likes to fail at tasks so I put a lot of time and effort into helping Carl. (I now refer to it as "Operation Save the World," because it was such a huge unattainable task that I took upon myself.) Of course, at the time I didn't realize a person can only help themselves if they truly want to change. I was willing to sacrifice anything and everything because this was "the man I loved," and we were destined to be together forever.

I don't remember exactly when the violence became so intense. He never hit me, so I didn't actually consider it abuse. My bruises were from his excessive pinching, shoving, kicking and hair-pulling. I distinctly remember one incident when I had all four wisdom teeth pulled and the two of us were watching a movie. I said something extremely insignificant and Carl lost his temper, so he began fiercely pinching my swollen cheeks together and slamming my head against the wall.

I was the helpless victim and would never fight back for fear of what else might happen. It soon became a sick cycle, but it always ended in tears and a dramatic apology, promising it would never happen again. Despite my swollen cheeks and the contusions on my head, he had never hit me, but the violence was now occurring more frequently and was getting worse each day. Soon I could barely get out of bed in the morning from my aches and pains, and no one knew how much I was hurting. He always made marks in places people couldn't see, and I always had good explanations if anyone happened to see. I was a tough girl, and I could withstand all this pain for "the man I loved." It wasn't the physical pain that hurt as much as the emotional pain that was tearing me apart on the inside.

On the exterior, my life seemed composed and everyone thought our relationship was perfect. Carl had even bought me a diamond engagement ring. He would constantly send me flowers at school and all the girls would always exclaim, "I wish I had a boyfriend like Carl. You're so lucky." Little did they know.

I don't know what made me finally realize that this treatment was inhumane. Maybe it was that my three best friends would no longer speak to me, or that my parents wouldn't listen to me. I was convinced that no one would be there for me if I didn't have Carl. I had become so exclusive and Carl was the center of my life. I do know that God played a role in helping me realize that what Carl was doing was wrong.

One Sunday morning, exactly two years after I began dating Carl, my family and I were sitting down at the breakfast table, and I broke down—it all came out. That was probably the most difficult moment of my life, but also one of the best, even though I didn't think so at the time.

I broke off all ties with "the man of my dreams" and began to piece my life back together. I started going to therapy. At first I thought I would die without Carl, but it only took time, lots of it, to change that. My family and friends were very supportive. They let me back into their lives after I had shut them out completely. I could not have done it without them.

A few months later in my behavioral science class, I had to do an oral exam on a social issue that is prevalent in our society. My speech consisted of my experiences with dating violence. The entire class was in tears even though most of them could not understand my experience. It felt good to come out of my corner of isolation, yet at the same time, it was also very scary. Most people don't understand fully unless they have been in a similar relationship. I was often asked, "Why would you stay in such a relationship and let someone treat you like that?" It's extremely difficult when people judge me in this manner, but it's part of my experience and has shaped who I am today.

I have now moved on to new responsibilities and greater aspirations of college life. I have become more independent and happy, thanks to all of the love and support from my family and friends. It's still difficult to learn to trust people, but I am thankful to all those who are learning and growing with me. I couldn't have asked for more than my supportive family, understanding friends and incredibly patient new boyfriend.

Last week I was checking my e-mail and I received this:

Dear Jenny,

I found your e-mail address in a student directory, and I decided to write you since I never got the chance to thank you for your presentation in our class about dating abuse. This summer I was looking at the handout you gave everyone about the signs of abuse. I begin hysterically crying as I realized that my boyfriend matched all too many of the signs. I knew it was a bad relationship, but I could not tell anyone and I thought it was my responsibility to fix it. After hearing your experience, I realized I couldn't. Your story gave me a lot of strength to get out of the relationship before it got worse. Well, at least the story has a happy ending for both of us; we are very fortunate. Thanks again for having the courage to tell your story. You really helped me a lot, even though you didn't know it at the time.

"Operation Save the World" didn't fail after all. I did rescue someone.

Jennifer Winkelman

Like a Brother to Me

Aaron was good-looking, funny and a senior in high school when I met him my freshman year. We met during track and field. He ran cross-country, and so did I. He introduced himself to me as we were waiting for the coach to arrive one day, and from then on we were friends. There was something between us, something very special. We grew to be the kind of friends who shared everything. We developed an unbreakable bond.

One day as we sat by the track chatting away, Aaron turned to me. "I love you," he said.

I stopped. "You love me?" I asked. I didn't know what to say.

"No, not like that," he said. "I love you like a sister."

I looked at him and smiled. I knew exactly what he meant, because I felt it, too. "I always wanted an older brother," I said softly.

"Exactly!" He laughed. "I always thought it would be neat to have a little sis."

Aaron had so many friends, but I was someone special. He assumed an older-brother attitude and was always making sure that I was taken care of.

By the end of the year we were inseparable, and I was sad to say good-bye soon. Aaron was off to college, and I would have to stay behind in high school.

"I'm going to miss you a lot," I said. "Promise you'll remember me."

"Don't worry," he smiled. "I'm planning on kidnapping you and taking you to college with me." We both laughed, and he assured me that he'd visit often and arrange for me to visit him on campus.

The last few days of track practice, Aaron wasn't there. I figured that he had a bad case of senioritis and was just slacking off. I wasn't worried.

"Paula," a voice called out one day after school, but it wasn't Aaron's. The voice belonged to Serbon, Aaron's best friend. "I have to tell you something." His voice trembled as he spoke. "Aaron's in the hospital with leukemia." He stopped.

I stared, speechless. It was impossible. Only last week we were running together. I wanted to scream and cry, but I couldn't move.

Aaron was put in the hospital and treated for cancer. I visited him in the hospital as often as I could. Slowly he got better, and I became hopeful. Death wasn't for Aaron. Not my brother. He had such a passion for life. He was real, and real people don't die.

A few months later, Aaron was released from the hospital, although college would have to be postponed. Unfortunately, his release was temporary, and pretty soon he was back in the hospital.

"Am I going to die?" Aaron looked up at me from his hospital bed. I looked into his clear blue eyes and saw something I had never seen before: fear. I paused for a moment. I knew that I had to be strong for Aaron because he had always been strong for me.

"Of course not," I laughed, holding back tears. "You're

going off to college in the fall, and I'm booking you for a date to the beach this summer!" He smiled. I stayed with him for three hours that day. I didn't want to leave his side. I wanted to make sure that he knew that I was there for him. When I finally left, I told him not to forget that he promised me a date this summer.

Aaron passed away a week and a half later. It was too unreal. Aaron wasn't supposed to be dead, but he was. Reality had replaced fantasy.

Aaron has been dead only a few months now, but I don't think of him as gone, not Aaron. He's still my big brother, and he still watches over me, making sure I'm okay. Sometimes when I'm out running, I hear Aaron's voice in the wind, laughing and telling me to keep going. He's right behind me.

Paula Leifer

I Will Be Missing You

You were so full of life,
Always smiling and carefree.
Life loved you being a part of it,
And I loved you being a part of me.

You could make anyone laugh,
If they were having a bad day.
No matter how sad I was,
You could take the hurt away.

Nothing could ever stop you,
Or even make you fall.
You were ready to take on the world,
Ready to do it all.

But God decided he needed you,
So from this world you left.
But you took a piece of all of us,
Our hearts are what you kept.

Your seat is now empty,
And it's hard not to see your face.
But please always know this,
No one will ever take your place.

You left without a warning,
Not even saying good-bye.
And I can't seem to stop,
Asking the question why.

Nothing will ever be the same,
The halls are empty without your laughter.
But I know you're up in heaven,
Watching over us and looking after.

I didn't see this coming,
It hit me by surprise.
And when you left this world,
A small part of us died.

I remember you swinging from the hayloft ropes,
When you were just a boy.
And the last time I ever saw you,
You were driving your pride and joy.

Your smile could brighten anyone's day,
No matter what they were going through.
And I know every day for the rest of my life,
I will be missing you.

Sara Profitt

Tag

I feel the capacity to care is the thing which gives life its deepest significance.

Pablo Casals

"You're it!" I screamed while slapping my classmate, Hunter, on his right shoulder. It was a kind of ritual to play tag at recess. Even in third grade, social standing was critical and tag was just another way of proving yourself. I wasn't too fond of the game. I'm not saying that I wasn't good, but it was rather tiring.

About ten minutes into our ritual, my attention was brought to the kickball field. A group of kids were huddled in a circle shouting malicious names. Curious to see who the poor victim was, I started to make my way over. As I was getting closer to my destination, our teacher Mrs. Smith started to get involved.

"What's going on here?" Mrs. Smith asked in a stern voice.

The circle was immediately broken and there sat a short, brown-haired girl. Mrs. Smith's eyes studied the crowd for a moment and then, bending down, she started to help the girl to her feet.

"Are you all right, sweetheart?" Mrs. Smith asked in a softer tone. The girl nodded and then began to walk away. "Would you all like not to play at recess for the rest of the year?" The children remained silent.

"Then stop tormenting Angelina. She's done nothing to harm you," Mrs. Smith said. "If I ever see any of you teasing her again, I will double your homework and you won't see this playground until next year. Do you hear me?"

"Yes, Mrs. Smith," the children said in unison. Just as it had started, it was over. None of the kids who were involved in the attack had any remorse. They quickly restarted their game as if nothing had happened.

I began to survey the area to see where the girl had gone. Her name sounded familiar, but I couldn't figure out where I had heard it last.

"Tag! You're it!" Hunter yelled.

"Can't you see I'm not playing anymore?" I said, irritated.

"You can't just stop playing. You're breaking the rules," he argued.

"Well, guess what? I just did," I said with a smirk on my face.

"You're a butthead," he responded cruelly.

"I am not!" I shouted. "Hey, do you know who that Angelina girl is?" I asked, changing the subject.

Hunter glanced at her. "That retard?"

"Yeah, didn't she used to be cool or something?" I asked, staring at her.

"She used to be until her mom died. After that, she got really stupid and quiet," Hunter said, trying to squish a grasshopper he had found in the grass. "You're not going to go play with her, are you? 'Cuz if you do that, you'll become stupid, too, you know. Stupidness rubs off on people. Well, that's what my dad tells me."

"I don't want to play with her. I was just asking," I said pitifully. After a moment of thinking, I turned around and hit Hunter in the back. "You're it!" I screamed as I bolted away toward the sandbox with Hunter close behind.

Spring was coming in full bloom. The flowers were starting to come alive, the trees were waking from their dark spell and the sky was finally clear and a beautiful blue. As the bus sped away, I took in a deep breath of fresh air. As the sweetness filled my lungs, I smiled and walked through my front door.

My mother was sitting on the floor filling out paperwork, while my brother was on the couch eating a peanut-butter sandwich. I dropped my book bag and headed for the kitchen.

"Hey, Hon," my mom said softly. "How was your day?"

"Good, I guess," I said, kneeling down to find the peanut butter in the cabinet.

"I have to tell you something," she said quietly.

"What is it?" I asked, not even looking at her. I found the peanut butter and placed it on the table. She was silent for a moment, then began to speak.

"As you know, I went to the doctor the other day. He did a lot of tests because of some problems I've been having," she explained. "Well, the doctor called today. The cancer is back." I immediately stopped what I was doing. At the time, I didn't know a lot about the disease. My grandfather had died of cancer a few years before, and as soon as I heard the word come out of her mouth, I thought of death.

I ran out of the house in tears. My mother followed me to the porch. She embraced me and cradled me in her arms. "Erin, it's gonna be all right. Dad's going to come home, and I'm going to start taking medicine that's going to get rid of it," she said reassuringly. I look back at that moment in astonishment at how confident and determined she was.

I was relieved when my father came walking through

the door. He was the strong one, the man of the house. But you could tell just by looking in his eyes, that he was petrified.

My mom had gone through cancer once before in 1988. She had gone to several doctors to find out why she wasn't feeling well. They did many CAT scans and tests, but all of them came out negative. After months of searching for the answer, they discovered what was going on. She had ovarian cancer.

I cried a lot during that time. I was so confused about the whole situation. I felt betrayed by God. I remember asking over and over why it had to happen to my mother. I even asked my mother. She would always just say that "everything happens for a reason," or that "good always comes out of every situation."

Meanwhile at school, I became distant from my friends. I would try to play games, but I would get frustrated and quit. I was starting to get ridiculed by even my closest friends.

"Why don't you ever want to play anymore?" Hunter asked me one day while I was sitting down watching a game of tag.

"'Cuz I don't want to, all right? Just leave me alone," I said angrily. I felt bad for yelling at him, but he didn't know what I was going through. He couldn't even conceive of it. Hunter looked at me, rolled his eyes and left to go play.

Days went by, then months, and soon my mother was back to the doctor for another appointment. She came home and told us the great news: She was allowed to stop her treatment. She was in remission for the second time. I began to feel like myself again.

Recess had just begun when I walked up to Hunter. He

turned to me just as I tickled him in the stomach and said, "You're it!" He gave me a huge smile and started to chase me. I had never laughed that much before. I was relieved. It was over; my mother was back.

"Ha! You can't catch me!" I screamed. I ran until I couldn't breathe. I bent down to catch my breath, and as I started to get up, my attention was again focused on the kickball field. There was another circle being formed, and in the middle was Angelina. I gathered up my strength and ran over.

"Leave her alone," I hollered.

I quickly turned around. Mrs. Smith was standing behind me. "All of you inside," she scolded. She looked at me and smiled. Then she started to follow the kids inside the school.

I looked at Angelina, smiled and started to walk away.

"My mother used to call me her little angel," I heard a voice say quietly in a sweet whisper.

"My mother calls me Baby Bear. She had cancer, but she's better now," I said, turning around so I could face her.

She took her eyes off the ground and said, "My mother had cancer, too, but she died last spring." I stared at her. Her eyes were plagued with the innocence only a young child has when she's lost the only thing dear to her.

"Hey, would you like to play tag with me?" I asked with a smile on my face.

"No, that's all right," she said.

I started walking toward the sandbox. As I was looking at the playground to find Hunter, I felt a tap on my shoulder. I quickly turned around and saw Angelina with the biggest smile on her face. Her soft green eyes were no longer dark and empty, but instead filled with light and hope. She looked at me and said, "You're it."

Erin Gandia

Eternal Light

No winter lasts forever; no spring skips its turn.

Hal Borland

Three years ago my best friend, Stephanie, was killed on her way to school in a head-on collision. The man who killed her did not have a driver's license and was under the influence. He was driving about sixty miles per hour and didn't even brake before he crossed into oncoming traffic and hit her. She died on impact. She was only sixteen. Painfully alone, somewhere between emotional inertia and complete despair, I struggled to navigate my suddenly unraveled reality.

When I received notice that my mother was at school to see me that foggy March day, my stomach sank. Something was terribly wrong. I immediately turned in my half-finished math test and rushed to the administration building to look for my mother. I found her sitting in the school's parlor. She asked me to sit—I stood. When she told me the tragic news, I could hear my heart pounding. The red walls seemed brighter then, and more fluid, as if they were swirling around me. A peculiar emptiness overtook me that afternoon in my mother's car as I repeated the words she had spoken to me earlier: *She died today. She died. She's dead.* I tried to make myself believe what I soon realized was the dark and horrific truth: Steph was dead, and she was never coming back.

There was a drastic change in my expectations and hopes for the future from that day forward. Never had I imagined that someone with whom I had cried, someone who had been a sister to me through everything from my parents' divorce to my first kiss—my future maid-of-honor—would no longer be in my life. All that was left of my future now were the questions. Who would give me those enormous, suffocating hugs and mischievous grins? What would I do at the times when her laugh was the only thing that could make me smile? Who would catch me when I fell? Who would be there for me when I endured the most crushing experience of my young life— the death of my best friend?

I had never felt so alone, and consequently I chose to look within myself for comfort and understanding. I hoped that somewhere, deep inside of me, she was still there and would guide me through the monumental changes occurring in my life. But as I began to peel back layers of my own consciousness, my feelings of isolation and desperation only grew. I had always considered myself a strong person, but I felt completely lost. I could not focus on my schoolwork or much else in my life except Stephanie's death. Most of my days were spent merely existing with little pleasure or interest in anything. I wrote poetry in math class and scrawled overly dramatic statements like "Have you ever lost yourself?" on my notebook during advanced placement biology. I never bothered or cared about the actual class discussion. I spent what seemed to be an eternity staring into the eyes of my favorite pictures of Steph. I had every lash and sparkle of those celestial blue eyes memorized, but I feared that my memory of the passion and charisma that I searched so intently for within them would fade. Although I didn't cry much, I thought a lot. I tried to figure out why she was gone, how someone could kill another person and have no remorse, what I was going to do with my life. Then, after much thought, I found something. Under all the layers of pain and frustration, something within me briefly twinkled.

A few months after Stephanie's death, her sister gave me a letter that she had found deep in one of her cluttered drawers. This letter was the healing catalyst I so desperately needed. She told me in the letter that she loved me always, that I was her best friend, and lastly, that I was her mentor. Like a piece of stardust, something deep inside of me began to illuminate my soul. Never in my life had I been so flattered, so touched, or felt so loved; it was as though she had left the letter behind to console and encourage me. She had always taken care of me before, and now I knew that her death did not change that. I realized that despite my suffering, I needed to take responsibility, use my talents and participate actively in my life's unfolding.

Now, whenever I'm worried, I ask her for guidance, and I swear that she has helped me profoundly. Whether she gives me the strength to call back after I've hung up on someone or the inspiration to trudge through my advanced placement language test with confidence and clarity, I know she helps me every day. Although it is impossible to verbalize such an abstract, warm confidence, I feel her presence inside of me as I succeed, and more importantly as I cry, longing for her sweet, warm embrace. It is with her strength and support that I am able to forge on in life. I have faith in her presence, and I have faith in myself.

Steph's death caused me to question myself and my

own position in life. I now feel that although I have endured an emotional darkness more intense and shattering than most eighteen-year-olds have, it is not the pain that has changed me, but rather Stephanie's love and confidence in me that has inspired my metamorphosis. I can feel her guiding light in my own life as it changes, and thus I have the courage and resilience to embark on a new chapter of my life. I emerge from the darkness as a confident, faith-filled young woman with an especially bright twinkle in her eye.

Anastasia

One Final Lesson

One rainy day I was at home playing on my computer when the phone rang. It showed up on my caller ID as one of my really good friends from across the state. I anxiously grabbed for the receiver and answered. But instead of the lively reply that I had come to expect from my friend, I heard nothing but sobbing. She was crying so hard she couldn't even talk. Finally, she got it all out. Two of her best friends had just died. Slowly over the next hour and a half I got the story piece by piece.

After I hung up I couldn't clear my mind of what I had just heard. It was a scenario I had heard too many times in my life. So I pulled the facts together and wrote a story of what happened. The following is what I came up with.

The last day of school is today. It couldn't be more perfect since today is also your seventeenth birthday. All that you and two of your buddies have planned is a night out on the lake.

For a couple of hours you and your friends sit in a little aluminum boat in the middle of the lake under the colorful skies painted by a setting sun. As you guys empty can after can from a case of beer, you talk about the usual: girls and your plans for the summer, and what it's going to be like when school begins and all three of you are finally seniors.

You don't notice the wind beginning to pick up, churning the calm, smooth lake into something dangerous. By the time you realize it's time to come in, the waves have already begun to thrash your little boat. Your friend gets the engine going and handles the steering while you work the throttle. As soon as he gets the engine started you open the throttle maybe just a little more than you should. With a jolt, the little boat is sent speeding across the waves. Halfway to the landing you helplessly watch in horror as you notice a huge wave coming at you from the side. Your friend turns the boat into the wind and toward the wave as you throttle down the engine for all you're worth, but not soon enough. The wave hits the boat at an angle, sending her off the crest and smashing down into its trough. All three of you are knocked against the side as the force of the wave capsizes the boat and sends you all into the lake.

You kick for the surface, but your legs feel heavy and sluggish. It feels as if something is pulling you down into the depths. Your boots, now weighted by the water, are pulling you deeper and deeper into the darkness. As much as you try, the light of the surface becomes more and more distant. As your last few seconds of consciousness pass, you desperately try to pull your boots off. You tear at the laces, but they won't come undone. You panic, thrashing wildly, doing anything just for a breath of precious air. Before blackness consumes you, images of your friends and family swim through your mind. *No*, you think to yourself. *This isn't happening to me. I'm only a teenager. I can't die!*

And then, almost as an answer to your thoughts, you miraculously find yourself on the sandy shore—dry, warm and sober. You see one of your friends swimming toward the beach. You call out to him, but he doesn't respond. He pulls himself out of the lake and he stands there shivering as water drips from his T-shirt, looking at the overturned boat. He calls out for you and your friend. "Hey!" you yell as you walk over to him. "I'm right here." But he doesn't seem to notice. He calls out again, and again you give him your same response: "Hey! I'm right here!" You step in front of him, but his frantic eyes look past you, around you, and even through you.

Oh, God, he says to himself. *What have I done?* He takes a few steps backward, then turns and runs up the road.

"Hey!" you yell. "Hey, where are you going?!" But it's almost as if you had said nothing at all. You watch helplessly as he continues to run until he disappears from sight.

For a time all is silent. Ten minutes pass, then twenty. After thirty, maybe thirty-five minutes, a siren pierces the silence. At first you don't notice. But within minutes ignoring it is impossible. Down the road come a multitude of emergency vehicles, followed in short succession by cars and trucks, some of which you recognize as belonging to friends. As people jump out of their cars, you notice that your parents are there also. Your father walks somberly, while your mother sobs endlessly in his arms. You run over to your parents, yelling out to them, but they don't seem to hear. They pull an officer aside to talk, to find out what is going on. As you get closer you hear the officer say, "Ma'am, I'm sorry but your son's body is missing. We have called in helicopters to search the beaches with searchlights. Men on horseback have gone up to scan the cliffs . . . divers will come in tomorrow."

"But you don't need all them!" you yell. "I'm right here! I'm not dead! It's not supposed to happen to me!"

As the night draws to a close, the lake fills with more

and more boats. People from all over your little town are out on the water with flashlights, calling out for you and your missing friend. And no matter how hard you yell, no one seems to hear you. You walk by groups of some of your best friends, and even some of those people with whom you never really got along. Some of them are trying not to cry, yet holding those who are.

You watch your girlfriend crying and calling out for you as her friends try to comfort her. "Don't cry," your soundless voice says to her. "I'm not dead. I can't be. I'm only seventeen. This can't happen to me."

Night gives way to morning and no one has left—instead, more have come. Your mother is out on the dock. She has been there for nearly five hours. You watch as your father and an officer walk out to her, and you hear your father whisper, "C'mon, honey, it's time to go now." She breaks into tears while you try desperately to hold back yours. She won't go. Not until the body of her son is found. The flood of emotions hits you like a brick wall when the police have to sedate her in order to move her from the end of the dock. *This shouldn't be happening,* you tell yourself. *I'm only a teenager. I can't be dead.*

The names of you and your friend, which have been called out by rescuers all night long, are drowned out by the high-pitched roar of two army helicopters. Immediately, their searchlights pierce the fading darkness and begin sweeping over the lake and the beaches that surround it.

One of the searchlights passes over you; you put your arms in front of your face as the blinding light engulfs you. And then is gone . . .

You lower your arms and look around. The helicopters are gone. As are the police, medics and firemen. They are all gone. The boats that once carried searchers and their flashlights bob gently in their moorings at the dock. Your friends no longer sit on the shore, crying at the realization that two of their companions are forever lost.

Instead, the sun rises over the clear and pristine lake. The sky is blue, with not a cloud in sight. Your clothes ripple as a cool west wind slips beside you.

In a clearing you can see a small congregation of people. As you walk closer, each and every one of them becomes familiar—each of them a friend or a family member. There are two sections of folding chairs, all of which are occupied. Before them, beside a little makeshift podium, propped above a pile of flower bouquets, are two pictures—one is of your friend whom you never saw after the boat capsized and threw all three of you into the lake. You hesitate to look at the other picture because you already know—it's you.

As one friend leaves the little podium, another stands and takes his place. She speaks about what the two of you meant to her and how much she will miss you. One by one, friends and relatives come up to speak, each emphasizing how much you will be missed. And you sit there and watch, all the time not believing that it happened to you. That you died, even though you were still a teenager.

Noah Campana

The Bus Stop

Waiting at the bus stop
I shivered from the cold.
When you walked up
it seemed as if
you were outlined all in gold.
You asked me if my shivering
was out of cold or fear,
I said the cold, I'm not afraid
for you to stand so near.

Then you removed your jacket
and handed it to me,
I shyly refused your jacket,
embarrassed so, you see.
You put the jacket on my shoulders
and back a step you took.
"I'm Anna," I said extending my hand.
"Tobias," you said. We shook.

Day after day we stood,
waiting for the bus,
Not a single word spoken

by either one of us.
Until one day I turned to you
and bravely started to say,
"I have a crush on you, Tobias,
and also, by the way—"

As I started to tell you what it was
that was burning on my mind,
You told me that you liked me, too,
but the words were hard to find.
I smiled a smile that seemed to stretch
to both of my two ears.
The smiling and the happiness
erasing all my fears.

And now, my friend, you're dying
and there's nothing I can do,
But sit with you and hold your hand
and be forever true.
Last night while you were sleeping,
your soul just slipped away,
The many words that filled my heart
were impossible to say.
As I was cleaning out the drawer
that stood beside your empty bed,
I found a letter addressed to me
and heard your voice speak as I read.

My darling I am sorry that
I will have to leave so soon,
You know how much I love you
and I know you love me, too.
I hope you won't forget me
but please do try to move on,

I hope that you won't cry too much
when I am dead and gone.

Two silent tears slid down my face
and moistened both my cheeks,
I won't get over the loss of you
not for days, and not for weeks.
I continued reading the letter
that I held in both my hands,
My fingers numb as if they had
been wrapped in rubber bands.

Now I'm standing at the bus stop
where two years ago we met,
And as I stand here in the cold
I feel my cheeks start to get wet.
I don't think I will get over you,
never, not in any way,
Our anniversary would have been
two years ago today.

And on this lonely bus ride,
I sit alone without you near.
I hear a voice that may just be
the voice I've longed to hear.
The voice is from an angel
and his words are sweet and strong.
He tells me, "Life's a treasure.
Learn to love again. Move on."

And through the words he whispers
I finally start to see,
That although I'll always love you—
It's time to set you free.

Anna Maier

5

FAMILY
AND LOVE

If you would be loved, love and be lovable.

Benjamin Franklin

My Little Brother

A sibling may be the sole keeper of one's core identity, the only person with the keys to one's unfettered, more fundamental self.

Marian Sandmaier

It was a stormy Saturday afternoon when my mother took my five-year-old brother, Christopher, and me to a new enormous toy store she had read about in the newspaper. "So many toys," the advertisement had shouted in full and flashy color, "that we had to get a huge warehouse to fit them all!" Christopher and I couldn't have been more excited. We ran across the parking lot, through the cold and biting rain, as fast as our little legs could carry us. We left our mother outside to battle with the frustrating umbrella, which never worked when she wanted it to.

"Christine! I'm going to find the Lego section! There's a new pirate ship I want, and I have four dollars! Maybe I can buy it!" Christopher exclaimed and ran off excitedly. I only half heard him. I took a right turn and, to my wide-eyed delight, found myself in the midst of Barbie World.

I was studying a mini mink coat and doing some

simple math in my head when suddenly an earthshaking clap of thunder roared from the storm outside. I jumped at the noise, dropping the accessory to the floor. The warehouse lights flickered once and died, covering the stuffed animals, matchbox cars and board games in a blanket of black. Thunder continued to shake the sky and whips of lightning illuminated the store for seconds at a time, casting frightening shadows that played tricks on my mind.

Oh no, I thought, as my stomach twisted and turned inside of me. *Where's Christopher?* I ran up and down the aisles through the darkness, panic filling my small chest and making it difficult to breathe. I knocked into displays of candy and tripped over toys, all the while frantically calling my brother's name. I needed to know he was all right, but I could barely see. Tears of frustration and fear trickled down my face, but I continued to run. I found Christopher in the Lego aisle. He was standing alone, perfectly still, clutching tightly to the pirate ship set. I threw my arms around him and hugged him until he couldn't breathe. Then, I took his hand in mine and we went to find our mother.

Years later, on a beautiful Tuesday morning, I was leaving my computer class on my way to sociology. As I drove, the radio filled my ears with horrendous news: A hijacked plane had crashed into the Pentagon and two other planes had crashed into the World Trade Center. Fires, destruction and chaos echoed across the east coast from Washington to New York City. My first thought was of Christopher.

My brother had joined the Air Force just a year earlier, and he was stationed in Washington. I had grown used to seeing him for a few days every five months or getting 2:00 A.M. telephone calls just to let me know he was alive and well. But as the Towers collapsed and newscasters began to cry, I was overcome with the need to see Christopher, to hug him and make certain he was all right. I pulled over to the nearest pay phone and frantically dialed my grandmother's number. Christopher would call her to let the family know what was happening. The operator asked me to hold; it seemed as if everyone in the nation was on the telephone, trying to get through to loved ones. I felt the familiar panic steal my breath as I waited for a connection. Finally, I heard my grandmother's voice.

"He's fine. He's okay. They might have to move him out. He might be called to help somewhere in some way, but he's fine, Christine. He called and told us he was fine."

I spoke with my grandmother for a few more minutes. Boston was evacuating its tallest buildings. Schools were closing. Some workers were being sent home. All airplanes were grounded. The sky was silent and crystal clear. As I hung up the phone, I began to cry from relief. It was silly of me to worry about Christopher, I scolded myself. He was an adult. He stood 6'2" while I, his big sister, never hit 5'5". He could fit both of my hands into one of his. Christopher could take care of himself. But I realized at that moment that there is still a piece of my heart that will always run to try to protect him, no matter how big he may be or where in the world he is located. That same piece will always remember the five-year-old boy standing in the dark toy store with the pirate ship clutched to his chest, saying, "I knew if I just waited here, Christine, you would find me."

Christine Walsh

My Sister, My Enemy, My Friend

If your sister is in a tearing hurry to go out and cannot catch your eye, she's wearing your best sweater.

Pam Brown

It is eerily ironic that two people who share the same genetic makeup can be so drastically different while sustaining such a mutual dislike of one another. Sure, we have the same plain, straight brown hair, freckled noses and bright blue eyes. However, apart from that, it seems we are two complete and total opposites, two sparring discordant mortals absurdly sharing the same mother and father. Until a few years ago, I thought there existed only one phrase to adequately describe the situation of my sister and me: dumb luck. Now that we've both grown a little, I realize we are much more alike than anyone ever knew, and our relationship has transformed into a bond deeper than any I'll ever know.

I guess it's just the way we were raised. We were always very competitive. She was successful at everything she attempted, and I was always five years behind, hopelessly trying to catch up. I resented her for her excessive achievements: the way she always won the science fairs, the way she always received such glowing report cards, the way she always exhibited such poise and self-control in her sophisticated, mature demeanor. Wildness and obnoxiousness were my claims to fame, and my sister bitterly despised my annoying quest to be the constant center of attention. Growing up, we had more than our share of fights. She would give me bruises, then buy my silence with a Barbie doll. At night, I would sneak in and steal her stuffed animals. For thirteen years, we were literally enemies next door, every day providing a new and devious battle in our quest to conquer one another.

As I became a teenager, the gulf between us grew, and that tumultuous year that she was a high-school senior and I had just entered the seventh grade became the most arduous trial I'm sure my parents have ever endured. She was afflicted with near-adult conceit and I was tortured by post-child insecurity. Between the two of us, enough screaming and hair-pulling occurred to scar anyone for life. We both strived for the attention of our parents yet we both pushed it away, competing in a sport where neither of us knew the rules or even where the finish line was. To keep the peace, we became mutes in each other's presence. Acknowledging the tension but savoring the silence, we tried to avoid each other altogether and became absorbed in other activities to stay away from home. We were like two warring armies building a wall to temporarily stave off battle.

I don't really know exactly what happened that caused us to come together. There isn't one particular incident or event that sparked our reconciliation, just a process that slowly unfolded as she developed a life away at college and I developed my own life in high school. Maybe it was that we both matured, or that we finally reached a point where five years didn't make such a big difference in our ages. I'm not really sure, nor do I care. Ironically, now she's the only one with whom I share all my secrets, all my insecurities and all my most fervent dreams. She laughs at my unwavering, silly, boy infatuations, and helped me cry over my first broken heart. We've spent many a night discussing life, expectations, our parents and even God. It turns out that although our actions are incredibly different, our thoughts are remarkably the same. We are both afraid of failure. We are both afraid to be alone.

My sister is neither the enemy nor simply just another human being. She is a woman, a loyal companion and ultimately a part of me. She knows my life better than any other person in this world, and she has accepted me, weaknesses and all. Sometimes we laugh at the way we used to act and reminisce about the evil pranks we used to play on each other. There is an intangible bond that binds us together. Unfortunately, we didn't discover it until we lived apart. We are two souls sharing the same heart and forever holding hands.

Allison Thorp

Always There for Me

She takes my hand and leads me along paths I would not have dared explore alone.

Maya V. Patel

I look around my room, and I see hundreds of faces. All over my walls are pictures of smiling moments, dramatic moments, teasing and playful moments. They scream with character or whisper of adventure or mischief. They each have their own personality, but in many of them there is the same person standing right next to me, many times holding me up. She is my identical twin sister, Sarah.

Sarah and I have never been apart for more than forty-eight hours. From the moment we were born, she has been the bigger one, the stronger one, the one most likely to take the brunt of a conflict and shield me from pain. We have gone through every aspect of our lives together, but sometimes that doesn't make life all peaches and rosebuds.

Two years ago, Sarah and I started to board a plane for our cross-country trip to California. I thought my heart was going to pound right through my chest. I could hear the blood rushing through my veins as I saw my parents' faces get swallowed up in the hustle and bustle of the terminal. As we sat in our seats, it felt like adrenaline alone was going to propel me right off the runway. Just then, I felt a warm pressure on my hand. Sarah was holding it firmly while gazing out the window.

"Just grab my hand, Kelley," she said reassuringly. "It'll be okay." And I believed her. I knew she would never lie to me. I knew that, after it all, she would be there for me.

We've gone through even rougher times together. I was there right beside her last summer when her boyfriend of fourteen months broke things off so abruptly that neither she nor I had known it was coming. I watched her sob on the weather-beaten picnic table in the backyard and knew I couldn't just stand there. I could hear her cries between birdcalls and mosquitoes buzzing as I ventured out onto the grass. Coming along beside her, I felt my heart tear as I saw her red, swollen eyes and clenched fists. I pulled out a wad of Kleenex and offered it to her.

We didn't say anything for a while. I just sat beside her on the picnic table and listened to her raspy breathing. Nobody else knows her breathing. They haven't listened to seventeen years of it at night, while she's reading or watching a movie. Every breath she takes is a sign of the most profound and special friendship I've got. Having a sister as a friend has meant the world to me, but having a soul mate who knows every nuance of my spirit has allowed me to survive, to live and to be happy. She's there for me, and I have tried to be there for her, too. I think my sister says it best in the heart-shaped stained-glass sun catcher she gave me years ago. It says simply: "Chance made us sisters; hearts made us friends."

Kelley Youmans

The Bigger Man

Although I am the younger brother, I have always felt like my brother's keeper. Even now that Brian is seventeen and I am sixteen, I still watch out for him because, though chronologically I lag behind, my parents have encouraged me to take the nurturing role.

You are probably thinking that my brother is either mentally or physically handicapped—he is neither. I'm not sure if his "nature" was born or created. My mom has treated him like fine china ever since his birth. Maybe it's because there were problems with his delivery. She often recounts how the umbilical cord became wrapped around poor Brian's neck, and how he could have strangled on it had the doctor not rescued him with a Caesarean delivery. Although Brian went full-term, his tiny size reflected his future fragility within the family.

After Brian's birth, my mom grew more religious. She made all sorts of deals with God to watch over her tiny infant in exchange for her spiritual devotion. A year later, I was born. I was the quintessential bouncing baby boy. From the way my mom describes it, I practically walked home from the hospital and was eating solid food by the time I was a month old—probably raw steaks.

My mom saw my larger size and strong constitution as a sign from God that I was to be a kind of guardian angel for my older brother, Brian. It was not at all strange to see me reminding Brian to tie his shoes, or asking the waiter for another glass of water for him. No one ever thought our reverse relationship was odd, since by the age of five I was a head taller than him anyway.

I could never leave the house without my mom telling me to drag Brian along. He was smaller and fit in better, size-wise, among my group of friends. But defending and protecting him became tiresome. And then there were those luscious desserts my mom would bring home to fatten up poor little Brian. I would watch him longingly while he delicately sipped at chocolate milkshakes and critically picked at the strawberry cheesecakes I would have gladly scarfed down if given half the chance. And when my hand, through no power of my own, would drift toward a tempting slice, my mom would reprimand me, saying, "That's for Brian. You don't need that."

And so, though I loved my older brother, I began to resent him as well.

One day our school sponsored a pumpkin-carving contest. First prize was one-hundred dollars, and I knew just how I would spend it. There was a brand-new Sega game—Dungeons and Dragons—that I was dying to own. Realizing that my birthday and Christmas were nowhere in sight, I decided that the first-place stash definitely had to land in my pocket.

I ran out to the market and picked out the nicest pumpkin I could find. Then I set out to draw on the most gruesome face. In my third-grade mind, I had created a Pumpkin Freddy Krueger, of sorts. Now all I had to do was carve the face. That's when it dawned on me. With my big clumsy mitts I'd surely screw it up. I thought of Brian's smaller delicate hands and knew he was the man for the job.

I pleaded with Brian to carve the pumpkin, but wise fourth-grade businessman that he was, he asked for a cut.

"How does eighty-twenty grab you, Bri?"

"You mean eighty for you and only twenty for me? Forget it. It's either fifty-fifty or nothing."

Quickly doing the math in my head, I figured out that even if I split the first prize fifty-fifty, I'd still have enough cash for the game—and I knew this pumpkin had to win the grand prize. It was just so awesome. So, I gave in to Brian's demands.

With skillful hands Brian carved the blood-slashed face, and then we sat back to admire our handiwork. Together, we had created the goriest Halloween pumpkin ever, which I was sure nobody could deny.

Then the unexpected happened: We came in second. Unfortunately, second prize was only fifty dollars, and I needed every penny of that to buy the game. The day of the awards ceremony, the principal handed over the money to me because Brian was home sick with some fragile kid's illness like a cold or something equally pathetic.

God, I thought to myself, *if he really wanted to win, he would have been here today. And I need the whole check to pay for the game.* I was able to justify stealing the cash from under poor Brian's runny nose. With hardly a thought, I ran over to my friend Glenn's house and his mom drove us out to the mall to buy the game. I felt no guilt that night as Glenn and I pounded away on our controllers having the time of our lives.

That night when I got home, I found Brian lying on the couch watching TV.

"Did we win?" he asked.

I tried not to flinch as I stared down at his cheesecake-eating, milkshake-sipping face, and I answered, "No."

I hid the game over at Glenn's and never told anyone in

my family about it. I thought it was pretty pathetic anyway that Brian never found out. What a dork.

As Brian got older, he began to loosen up a little and Mom did, too. He actually had a growth spurt, and though I'm still a head taller than him, he's wider from side to side now—guess those milkshakes finally caught up with him.

With Brian's hearty physique and persistent begging, Mom even gave in to allowing him to attend college away from home. I played my usual role in helping him pack, although I had mixed emotions about seeing him go. I'd miss having the geek around.

As I rifled through one of his desk drawers, a photo of our gruesome pumpkin dropped to the floor. We both laughed as we looked at the ridiculous face we'd thought was so frightening. Then Brian said, "And we actually thought that squash was going to make us rich. We didn't even win third prize."

A kind of guilt rose up in my throat, and I felt a confession of sorts was needed.

"Brian, uh . . . hate to admit this, but we kinda did win. In fact, we kinda won second place."

"Huh? Is that so?" he said scratching his head. Brian rustled through his desk drawer again and pulled out another photo of our pumpkin with a blue satin second-prize ribbon flanked across its bloodstained face.

"I took this the day after the contest, Worm Brains. What did you think, I didn't know? I was the photographer for the school newsletter, Einstein."

"What? You actually knew and didn't say anything? Why?"

Brian looked down at his half-packed suitcase, and then up at me. "Don't you think I knew how Mom always forced you to watch out for me, and don't you think it made me feel really small? I'm supposed to be the bigger brother, Numb Nuts."

Actually, I'd never thought about how Brian might feel; it just always felt like I was the one being put out. Everyone always seemed to care more about Brian. Everyone needed to protect poor, pathetic Brian—I was just the big, dumb bodyguard for hire.

"I wanted, just once, to do the same for you," Brain said, interrupting my thoughts. "Just once, I wanted to be the bigger man."

"It always looked to me like it would be way better being smaller," I confessed. "I wanted to be the one who everyone wanted to take care of."

"You're such a jerk," Brian said, shaking his head. "Do you know how lousy it feels when everyone thinks you're so lame you can't even take care of yourself? It sucks!"

We sat silently on Brian's bed, just staring at one another. As dense as we were, something finally sunk in. How pathetic. We'd each lived our lives secretly wishing to be the other.

"I'm sorry, Bri," I mumbled.

"For what? About that pumpkin? Forget it."

And then another uncomfortable silence lay upon us. I wanted to tell Brian how much I loved him and how cool I thought he was. But I felt really dumb saying it out loud. Then Brian kneeled over, scooped up his football and threw it at my head. I lunged for him and pounded him in the gut. This was the way we communicated our understanding.

C. S. Dweck

A Pyramid

We do not remember days; we remember moments.

Cesare Pavese

My mother's grating demands finally became too much this summer, so I submitted to "really cleaning my room." I excavated everything I'd stashed and put out of the way for years. I gutted and sorted countless vaults jammed with old erector set models, souvenir Kennedy Space Center pennants and long-forgotten rock classification science projects. Mired in the habitual rearrangement of my junk, I planned to just empty and repack the containers to satisfy my mother and to free some time for leisure. As the dust started to settle, I realized I was completely surrounded by treasures saturated with priceless memories and sentimental value. Each item urged me to save it and put it in a safer place—my museum of precious trinkets atop my bookcase. I bulldozed the garage from the neater display of more worthy pieces and came upon a wrinkled plastic bag containing two three-dimensional puzzle pieces resembling oddly-cut jewels of opaque turquoise plastic. A smile spread across my face as I remembered my first experience with this seemingly insignificant, peculiar-looking relic from my childhood.

When I emerged from the toy-enhanced world of an eight-year-old's room and into the kitchen, I noticed my father hunching over the table, his full attention on the objects he was growling at in his hand. His focus was evident; he did not even pause from his task to glance up at my entrance into the room. His brow was furrowed in deep thought and glowed with frustration in the yellow light. Hoping to get his attention and offer my help, I boldly climbed into his lap, thrust my curious face into his and asked, "What are you doing?"

He surrendered his concentration and explained the source of his annoyance and the focus of his attention for the past thirty minutes. "I'm trying to build a pyramid from these two little pieces. It's sort of a three-dimensional puzzle." Perched on his knee, I picked up the two wedges and stared at them, admiring their peculiar shape and hypnotizing color. My father scooped me up, rose and set me back down all in one fluid motion—a feat accomplished only by dads. "I'm just going to go to the bathroom," he stated. As the bathroom door down the hall closed, I immediately began building—arranging the pair of pieces, rotating them, leaning them together—until I slid one piece on top of the other laterally and staring at me was a diminutive plastic pyramid. I yelled, "I got it!" and giggled with delight.

An incredulous "What?" erupted from the bathroom as my dad came stumbling out in the process of pulling up his pants. Like a royal monument, a miniature pyramid stood triumphantly on the table, and the expression of surprise, disbelief and envy upon my father's face was both priceless and unforgettable.

As I sat there Indian-style in my dusty room this past August and toyed with this little souvenir of my childhood, I dreamily examined my relationship with my father and the person he was, sifting through my memories. I remembered all those summer evenings before dinner when I watched the Weather Channel with him, listening to him explain the Gulf Stream, the barometer and those windy condition sailboat symbols that looked like chickens. I recalled the excitement in his dark eyes and in his energetic voice as he studied the cold and warm fronts, making his own personal forecast on the upcoming weekend's weather while deciding if we would all visit my grandmother on Long Island and the nearby beach. I remembered his approving nod when I understood and his later satisfaction when he lounged in his beach chair under the gleaming sun like a triumphant pharaoh.

My father seemed most at home at the beach. His tanned face would relax while his eyes would scan the sand and water with the experience of someone who had grown up there. He just knew when the water would be safe for swimming and sensed when and where riptides or sandbars would develop. One time, to get past the crashing waves so I could play in a tidal pool, he carried me on his shoulders. He made sure my mother, sister and I always had a thick layer of sunscreen on to protect us from the sunburns he had received as a kid. We'd bury each other in vast tombs of sand, adorning them with shells and gems of sea glass. Our sand castles and the holes we dug were legendary all over Long Island. So were the intense games of paddleball and the unruly battles with rock-stale donut holes.

A jagged half-inch scar just below my dad's eyebrow served as a lesson to never hide the truth from those you love. As a headstrong teen, he lied to his mother and went surfing, and the sharp tip of his surfboard gashed his face.

He hid the evidence of his guile with a Band-Aid, feeling guilty and predicting the consequences of its discovery, besides the stitches he should have received. The mark never went away, but it captured my dad's experience and the colorful, fascinating life he led—and the many adventures he had along the way.

My dad and I shared so much, especially a zest for life. His desire to share his knowledge with me, to challenge me and to teach me never ceased. Intelligence and wisdom radiated from his expressive face anytime he became excited, which was often. I never saw someone become so ecstatic over a science project that labeled the parts of the human heart. My youthful vigor and intelligence fascinated him, and the awe and pride in my father's eyes inspired me. We helped each other to really live. His presence, along with my mother's, was the security and stability of my life—the foundation upon which I built my own pyramid.

As I looked around my room, scanning over the relics from the first seventeen years of my life, I realized I was smiling. Now, I was piecing together my own pyramid, living by my dad's lessons, adding my own uniqueness, creating a mysterious whole from parts of a puzzle, as my father would have wanted me to as he watches from heaven. In my hand was a priceless symbol of our relationship. Although we are separated like the two pieces, my dad and I will always form a perfect pyramid— together.

Jonathan Evans

Of Fathers and Sons

I wasn't brave enough to get a tattoo—I'd considered getting a field mouse swimming for his life with a large-mouth bass surfacing to swallow him whole—so I got a removable platinum post pierced just below my lower lip. The guy who installed it said not to get silver or gold for anything that goes near the mouth or teeth. "Too soft," he said. "And you don't want to poison yourself."

Dad was a bit peeved. Okay, Dad was a *lot* peeved. He said I looked like I'd joined an Amazon tribe and why hadn't they just made the hole big enough to hold a Pepsi. "Supersize it," he said. My dad is always making jokes, tacking some quote about George Bernard Shaw on the end of them: *He was never more serious than when he was joking.* It's my dad's way of dealing with things that make him uncomfortable.

"You don't have to take me to bridge group," I said.

"When did *you* take up bridge?" he asked.

"No, I mean . . . "

"I know what you mean," he said and walked into the kitchen.

"Did you see that?" he asked my mother.

"It's a phase," she said. That's how *she* deals with

everything. *This too shall pass;* that's *her* quote.

I make decent grades—Bs. Could be worse. I'm no star athlete, but I'm not a serial killer, either. I didn't make Eagle Scout, but I'm not into drugs. I'm not a straight edge, but I don't drink and drive. I don't have any problems that are going to get me into any real trouble, something I can't say about a lot of the kids in my class. Don't get me wrong, I'm not saying they're going to end up in prison—statistically, I guess a few will have to—but I do think I'm a lot closer to the straight and narrow than a lot of them. My fantasy is to throw a big party for everyone with bigger troubles than me. Invite them over to my house. Make my dad meet them.

I'd introduce him to Malcolm. Malcolm's father is a clergyman, and Malcolm thinks it is some kind of preordained, cosmic fate that he'll spend his whole life getting into trouble. Malcolm once went out into the country and shot a skunk, climbed up on the roof of the school and tossed it into the ventilation system. School was canceled for a day and Malcolm was suspended. (He just had to tell someone—it wasn't me, if that's what you're thinking—and word traveled pretty fast.) The principal asked why he did it. "To express myself," he said. I think if my dad knew about Malcolm, he wouldn't mind my post so much.

Then there's Sheila, who blew the doors off the PSATs and had Ivy League schools calling her house. Sheila has no interest in college; her parents made her take the exams. Most kids would fail them just to tick off their folks, but Sheila was too clever for that. She set some kind of new school record for the PSAT and then expressed herself by telling the people from Stanford that she'd love to come but would be busy serving forty-to-life. That sent her folks up the wall. Sheila wants to be a cop, but for some reason that's not good enough for them. Personally, I think she'd make a fine cop.

I'd also introduce Dad to the smoking-lounge kids. It seems that half of them are pregnant; Dad could see that I'm not pregnant or a smoker. I've only got a post. And it's platinum. He'd of course point out: *You're male! How're you going to get pregnant?* And he'd have me there. But it's good to concede a point now and then.

All I've got is a piece of metal puncturing my skin. It's not hurting anyone else. I get some strange looks, of course; in fact, maybe that's why I did it. My dad keeps asking me why, and I just don't know. Maybe I'll take a cue from Sheila and make something up. Maybe I'll tell him I just did it to get his attention. That's not true, of course; he always has time for me. But we could share a good laugh just the same.

"How do you eat with that thing in?" Dad wants to know.

I shrug as I shovel in a fork full of green beans. It's a good question. Food buildup around it is a problem and buying a Water Pik wouldn't be a bad idea. But it's a rhetorical question. He's playing tennis now, serving me a lob, which I'm supposed to bat back.

"Good thing you don't have to send photos for college applications." He doesn't let up.

"I could take it out around the house," I offer.

"Now there's a start."

"But then what would you have to criticize?"

"Your haircut for starters."

I know he loves me. I know he respects me. He wouldn't bother giving me a hard time if he didn't.

"The world has changed since you were a kid," I tell him.

"More TV channels. That's all."

"You know something, Dad?"

"What's that, Son?"

"I love you."

He looks me up and down a bit suspiciously. It's the line that always gets him. The looking me over is all part of his act. "I know," he smiles and turns his attention to his plate.

"So the post isn't so bad, after all, is it?"

"It's very nice. Very much in vogue," he says. "If you live in the rain forest."

Scott Diel

A Confession

I was watching you sleep the other day,
And prayed that it would last.
The peace that rested on your face,
I'd never seen in the past.

I was watching you speak a while ago,
And hoped that you'd go on.
The way your words, they had no end,
Your spirit seemed so strong.

I was watching you fight the other day,
And prayed my tears would dry.
All this, I knew was done for me,
And couldn't figure why.

I was watching you smile a while ago,
And stared in total awe.
Was it me who made you shine?
Was that triumph that I saw?

And all this time you've waited,
And all this time you've helped.
And all the things you sacrificed,
For me to grow up well.

And all the tears you dried,
And all the pain you soothed.
And all the truths you had to hide,
Without a simple thank-you.

But I was watching you the other day,
And I realized I can't wait.
To tell you how much I appreciate,
And love you in every way.

Sami Armin

Journeys with Dad

Before I got my driver's license and spare time was so rare and precious, my father and I would sometimes go for drives. Before we would leave the house, he would pull out his old tattered map stained with coffee and rips along the edges and study it. I remember watching him sit at the kitchen table, bent over the rumpled paper, his spectacles clinging precariously to his nose. He always reminded me of a mad professor—he had the appearance and diligence of one.

After a while, I would hear a shuffling of feet. He would stand and, without saying a word, take the car keys from the dish where he kept them. He would walk briskly to the garage, a man on a mission—unstoppable, unpredictable. I would have missed him had my mother not called to me in an urgent voice, "Hurry, he's in the car!" In the garage, he would be sitting in the car, not saying a word, but not leaving, either. I sometimes wonder if he would ever have ever left without me. I doubt it.

On these infrequent trips, I remember my father permitting me to listen to the radio—a change from his typical "this is my car, I'm the one driving, and I want peace" attitude. With the radio blasting, we would hit the highway and follow it for only a few exits. Then my father would turn onto some unfamiliar back road (what he always called the "scenic route"). As we continued on our journey, me singing along with the radio, I would watch as the houses grew further and further apart. I would busy myself counting the number of basketball hoops in the driveways. In my eyes, they represented civilization. They were signs of life on these silent roads. To me, it was all "farm country." To my father, though, it was peace.

I took for granted those drives into the depths of upstate Connecticut. I took for granted even more the driving lessons he gave me on those quiet, bumpy, obstacle-course-like roads.

After I got my permit, he never once complained when I requested driving time. By then, I knew all of the roads and never had to use the map. Where I took him was my choice. I know he loved those rides. Sitting in the passenger seat gave him the opportunity to take in more of the surroundings. I think that he also took pride in my navigation abilities. He instilled them in me, after all. I am a product of him, and I think he saw that.

Now that I have my license, my father rarely joins me when I go out. I have my own places to go, he says, and he has his own license. I cannot forget, though, how he taught me to find my way, not only on the roads of Connecticut, but also on the roads of life. He showed me that a person can only prepare someone so much, and in the end, there will be no maps. I learned that there is reward, even if it is just peace of mind, in finding one's own way.

Caitlin Keryc

CLOSE TO HOME JOHN McPHERSON

© 1994 John McPherson/Dist. by Universal Press Syndicate

3-17

"My 17-year-old drove the car into the garage door
three times, so I finally just said the heck with it
and installed the beads."

In Mom We Trust

My mom embarrassed me. In fifth grade, she was the mom interrupting sex education with my birthday cupcakes. In seventh grade, she picked up the phone and told me it was bedtime at 9:30 on a Friday night when I was on the phone with Eric, the cute boy in art class. And after Sam stood me up on the night of winter formal, my mom stormed into his work and made a scene, demanding he pay for my unused dress and shoes. Although (I must admit) it would have been classic to see the look on his face had I been there, I was furious with her for making matters even more humiliating. Mom was always there to serve and protect. She was like a superhero who just seemed to make everything worse.

During the middle years when every month brought changes in bra size, boyfriends and hair color, my mom was as impossible to hide from as puberty. She was like a supernatural force, a divine spirit with psychic abilities. If I made any sort of mistake, she knew about it before I walked through the front door. She had a sixth sense, and it wasn't fair. My friends could experiment and lie and be out past curfew, and their parents would never in a thousand years catch on. As for me, if I were to even sample a beer or inhale one drag of a cigarette, my mom knew. As a result, by high school I had learned that it was best for me not to lie—after all, I knew better. I had a mom who knew everything, anyway.

And then there was a night when I couldn't be honest. All my friends were making a journey down to Mexico for the evening. The boy I especially liked invited me to come along. He was older and had a car. I really, *really* wanted to go. I had resisted in the past, but this time I found myself agreeing to the invitation. (My parents thought I was spending the night with my best friend.) We went, and it was fun and dangerous and stupid, and GREAT! Luckily, we made it home safely that night, and I spent the night at a friend's house. His parents weren't home, but if they had been, I have a feeling they wouldn't have cared that ten high-schoolers were gathered in their living room after a night in Tijuana. They were the type of parents who just didn't seem to care all that much about anything, which at the time I thought was pretty cool.

The morning after my little rebellious experience, my dad opened the front door to greet me.

"Hi Bec," he cheered. My mother put down her dish-towel and kissed me on the cheek. I waited for her to notice something different about me, something that might lead her to believe that I had been up to no good.

"I'm gonna take a shower now," I began.

She didn't say anything. She just hugged me tightly and asked me not to forget to clean my room. I spent twenty minutes in the shower wondering what I should do. My mom would surely figure it all out sooner or later. *Should I tell her?*

I decided to stay rigid. I was a good little actress. I could cover for myself if I needed to. A lie (just this once) couldn't hurt anyone. When I came down for breakfast, I waited for the inquisition, but to my surprise, it never came. Mom's crystal ball must have been cloudy that day, and for once, she didn't suspect a thing. I was in luck. I was relieved. I was shocked. I was *guilty*.

My conscience caught up with me after a few days. I couldn't stand it anymore and I told Mom everything, every detail. She cried, of course, scared for my life, afraid of what could have happened to me, and through her gentle tears she grounded me—for an entire month! Why, might you ask, did I tell her? Trust me, I asked myself that same question every day of that miserable month. I could have gotten away with it. I know that for a fact—or do I?

Sooner or later she would have probably found out about everything. And if that had happened, she would have not only grounded me, but would have lost all of her trust in me, as well. You see, after the Mexico incident, after I had confessed and then served my sentence, I eventually earned back my parents' trust. In return, I was given a later curfew, not to mention more privileges.

I didn't tell my parents *everything* after that. Instead, we had a system. I told Mom and Dad where I was going, when I would be back and the important things that were happening in my life. It turned out that superpsychic mom was cooler than I had originally thought. I liked that she cared about me and my life, and I really liked being able to share with her.

Over the years, Mom's embarrassment factor has dimmed like an old night-light, but she remains the raging superhero she always was. Even though I'm living one hundred miles away, she brings me soup if I'm sick, helps with my work when I'm swamped and makes sure that boyfriends are treating me right. She still has her crystal ball on hand and will often call me on a bad day to cheer me up even before I tell her that I was just fired, dumped or just plain lonely. She has grown to be my best friend,

and even though I don't live at home anymore, I still confide in her and tell her everything. Well—almost.

Rebecca Woolf

My Mother

My mother kept a garden,
A garden of the heart,
She planted all the good things
That gave my life its start.

She turned me to the sunshine
And encouraged me to dream,
Fostering and nurturing
The seeds of self-esteem.

And when the winds and rain came,
She protected me enough—
But not too much because she knew
I'd need to stand up strong and tough.

Her constant good example
Always taught me right from wrong—
Markers for my pathway
That will last a lifetime long.

I am my mother's garden.
I am her legacy,
And I hope today she feels the love
Reflected back from me!

Staci Warren

Broken Heart

Tears may be dried up, but the heart—never.

Marguerite de Valois

I was six years old when I experienced my first heart-break. The boy's name was Matthew. He was older than me, a cool eight-year-old. His hair was the color of beach sand and, as it blew in the wind at recess, his bangs would fall over his dark blue eyes in exactly the right way. He played touch football with his friends while I watched him from the tire swing on the playground.

"Someday I'm going to marry Matthew," I told my friend Nicole, as I pumped my legs, and my golden pony-tail flew behind me as I swung higher and higher.

Nicole sighed. She was my very best friend, content to follow me anywhere. It was always me who would drag Nicole along to a new adventure, her protesting and kick-ing, and me pushing on resolutely. I wasn't afraid of any-thing. Well, almost anything. I was terrified to let Matthew know that I had a huge crush on him.

I drew pictures for him every day at school. I liked to draw houses with big apple trees in the yard and a smiling yellow sun in the top corner. I dreamed of living in one of those houses with Matthew, where every morning we would go outside and pick apples from the tree and eat them for breakfast. My teacher, Madame LeBlanc, liked to look at my drawings.

"Très bien," she would say, admiring one as I stood by her desk, beaming with pride. *"C'est pour qui?"*

"Mon papa," I would answer, telling her it was for my father when in reality it wasn't. It was for Matthew, but I didn't have the guts to give it to him.

By the last day of the school year, I had made up my mind. Toward the end of the day, as jubilant and rowdy kids emptied out their desks and tidied up the classrooms, I quietly asked my teacher for permission to get a drink from the fountain. Behind my back, I clutched my very best drawing, with my name written in very small letters on the bottom.

I knocked on the door to the third-grade class. The teacher opened the door and peered down at me, a little first-grader with an earnest smile. She smiled back, looking mildly puzzled. She asked if she could help me with anything.

I thrust the picture at her. *"Pour Mathieu,"* I said, using the French version of his name. Then I turned and scampered back to my class. My palms were sweaty and my heart was beating. I wondered what he would think of my drawing.

The school bell rang then, and laughing kids poured out of the school, with weary but relieved teachers waving good-bye and telling them to have a good summer. I gave Madame a hug before I left and waved good-bye to my friends. My grandpa was waiting for me outside.

He grinned as I slid into the front seat and reached over to help me fasten my seat belt. His blue eyes twinkled. "How was your last day, Ashleigh?"

I shrugged. "Fine." My stomach was turning somersaults and I still felt awed at what I had done. However, I didn't want to talk about it with my grandpa. It was my secret.

Our car slowly crept along the driveway in front of the school, behind the big yellow school buses waiting to take kids to their summer freedom. Our car stopped right in front of the big steps leading to the front door. On them sat Matthew and another third-grader, a tough-looking girl named Alice with a messy black ponytail and dirt-smeared cheeks. Matthew was holding my drawing in his hands. My window was rolled down, and I could hear them laughing at it. A tear slid down my face, and I wished with all my heart that I had never given him that picture. My stomach felt like little green men were kicking it from the inside.

The car rolled forward, and we left Matthew and Alice behind. I could hear their cruel laughter ringing in my ears. Grandpa drove on in silence, glancing at me as I hunched up in a little ball on the seat, tears falling from my eyes.

"Ashleigh, what's the matter?"

I shook my head and a sob escaped. Out poured the story. Grandpa listened, trying hard to understand me through all my sobs and sniffling. He said nothing, just nodded and patted my knee.

"Come on," he said. "I'll buy you a milkshake."

Before long we were sitting in a booth, with me slurping on a vanilla milkshake and Grandpa stirring his coffee, deep in thought. He finally put down his spoon and took a sip. Looking me squarely in the eyes, he spoke.

"Ashleigh, I want you to know one thing and never forget it: I love you very much, and so does Grandma, and your mom and dad and your little brothers. No matter what happens, we will always love you," he explained. He took my small hand inside his larger, calloused one. "Forget about Matthew. He doesn't deserve you! You're a smart, pretty and kind little girl, and someday, a long time from now, you will meet somebody very special who will love you, too. But you have to wait for it, until you're grown up."

I stared into my milkshake. "But how will I know?" I whispered.

Grandpa squeezed my hand. "You'll know."

I nodded, and we got up and left the restaurant. Already I was beginning to think ahead. Nicole was coming over the next day, and we were going to go swimming at the pool. Maybe my little brothers would want to build sand castles in the sandbox when I got home. I had the whole summer before me. I had my whole future before me.

Ashleigh Dumas

A Simple Gift

I was fortunate enough to have a special person in my life who could light up my world. No, he wasn't famous (although everyone in our city seemed to know him). He wasn't the sort of person who stood out in any way. He was my Uncle Richard. Plain and simple. Though it wasn't clear to anyone else why he put a smile on my face every day, we both knew. He told me constantly that I was the most gullible girl in the entire world. I would deny it every time. I guess I was the perfect teasing target.

When I was about ten or eleven years old, I loved Slinkies. Boys liked Hot Wheels and footballs. Girls liked Barbies. I liked Slinkies. One day I was sitting on the floor in front of my uncle playing with my Slinky and he said, "Ya know, the best kind of Slinky is one that can go upstairs as well as down." At first I didn't believe him, but he somehow managed to convince me there was such a thing. So for about a year he had me looking for that perfect Slinky.

A few years slipped by and I grew out of my Slinky phase. Eventually, my uncle was diagnosed with cancer of the bone. At first he was strong, but it eventually took a toll on him. He was not somebody to go down without a good fight. One night I went to visit him in the hospital. I wanted to make him smile so I brought him a gift. I said, "I found the perfect Slinky. It goes both upstairs and down. But this one's smarter than the rest. It takes the elevator." I had never seen him laugh as hard as he did that day.

My uncle passed away a few years back. Today that Slinky lies on his grave as a reminder of what we both know: I am the most gullible girl in the world.

Shelby Schanandore

6

ACTS OF KINDNESS

You give but little when you give your possessions. It is when you give of yourself that you truly give.

Pierre Corneille

The Stranger Within

After the verb "to love," "to help" is the most beautiful verb in the world.

Bertha von Suttner

It was one of those sweltering, hot days in the middle of July when all you can do is dream of the cold winter days that you hated only months earlier. One of those sultry days when you either yearn for a swim in a pool or crave a cool drink. In my case, all my friends who had pools I could invite myself into were away on vacation, and the public pools were out of the question unless I could learn to enjoy suffocating myself in chlorine with hundreds of other delirious people. Instead, I decided to go to the neighborhood café where they sold my favorite dessert, frozen yogurt. Since my parents hadn't given me a car for my sixteenth birthday, the only option I had was to walk.

Dragging a friend along, we headed for the ice-cream shop, almost passing out from the burning heat of the angry sun on the way. As we trudged along, my friend continuously grumbled about the heat and why she had so foolishly decided to come with me on this hair-brained quest for frozen yogurt. I just shrugged, perspiration dotting my forehead, mumbling.

"We're almost there. Just think of cool air conditioning and the sweet taste of frozen yogurt on your tongue. It'll be worth the walk," I assured her.

I had to admit to myself that the café was quite a distance from our house. I was beginning to get extremely thirsty, and my head was reeling from the smoggy air.

When we were about a block away from the café, I noticed her for the first time. She was old, somewhere in her mid-seventies I guessed. She had this awful arch in her burly shoulders as if she couldn't hold the heavy weight of her large chest. Her curly hair was frizzy from the heat and dyed a horrible greenish-yellow, which was clashing dreadfully with her neon pink shirt. She was struggling, pushing a squeaking grocery cart full of what appeared to be beauty-salon items.

Besides all her extraordinarily gaudy clothing, her most dominant feature was the deep frown she wore. At first, I thought it was from the harrowing heat, but with each step toward us her scowl increased, creating a more disturbing picture of a very unhappy soul. It seemed as though she hated the very air she breathed, reminding me of the cantankerous lady who used to live on our street, the one my friends and I called The Witch.

I glanced at my friend to see if she had noticed her. I could tell she had, for she was wearing the usual disgusted face she wore when she disliked something and somehow felt superior to it. My friend was the type of person who was very conscious of what others might think of her. She wanted to remain flawless to the world so, when she was presented with someone who was different in any way, she became arrogant and condescending.

As we drew closer to the lady pushing the grocery cart,

my friend directed us as far away as she could, until we were nearly walking on the road. I began to observe the many others that were passing by. They, too, were avoiding her at all cost as if she were a leper or a criminal of some kind.

The lady stared blankly ahead, her wobbling knees hitting the sides of the cart. Somehow, I felt ashamed at my reaction, but that didn't stop me from hurrying by. Just as we made it past her, I heard this horrible sound from behind me and quickly turned around to see what it was.

The lady's cart had been knocked over and her soap, perfume and shampoos were scattered across the pavement. Shocked, I looked at the lady's hunched back trembling as she slowly bent with great care to begin collecting her items.

I gulped. Many things were running through my head. I looked at my friend inquiringly. "What should we do?" I asked quietly.

"What should we do? We shouldn't do anything!" my friend said, rolling her eyes heavenward.

"Yeah, I know, but it looks like she needs help," I responded softly as the lady began feebly assembling a couple of perfume bottles into her lap.

"Well, I'm sure she's okay. Someone else will help her. Besides, we didn't knock her cart over . . . ," my friend said with cold logic and then started to walk ahead. I stood there for a minute thinking. Something was tugging at the strings of my heart and, all of a sudden, I felt great compassion for this pitiful lady. At that very moment, I knew what I had to do.

"Are you coming?" my friend called over her shoulder impatiently.

"No, I'm going to help her," I said with determination as I began to head back toward the lady.

"What? Amy . . ." my friend groaned through clenched

teeth, giving me that look that said, *Don't test me, and don't expect me to follow you.*

I didn't pay attention to my friend as I cautiously knelt down beside the lady who was now furiously attempting to set her cart upright once more. I could feel the inquiring, skeptical eyes of the passersby. I knew they were thinking I was crazy for helping her or, worse, that I had clumsily knocked over her cart and therefore was assisting her out of duty.

"Here, let me help you," I said gently, as I began to position the cart upright.

The lady slowly glanced up, her large eyes filled with such fear, sadness and pain that I was frightened by her stare. I gulped and then, hesitantly, began putting the items back into her cart.

"Go away," she grumbled, throwing a tube of cream into her cart. "I don't need your help."

Shocked, I backed away from her seething stare and looked up at my friend who was haughtily standing by, glaring with her arms folded smugly against her chest. I sighed.

"No, I want to help you," I continued, putting three more shampoo bottles into the cart. The lady peered at me as though I was crazy. Maybe I was, but I knew that I was supposed to help her. She didn't stop me this time so I helped her put away the rest of her items. I was stunned by how many people walked by and hopped over certain disarrayed items in their paths, not even offering a sympathetic word or glance. What astounded me even more was when a cute guy whom I had liked for as long as I could remember was one of the uncaring, selfish people who strolled by. I was embarrassed by his reaction when he first saw me in a humiliating situation and then disgusted by his self-centered attitude.

When the last item was put back into the cart, I slowly

rose to my feet, flinching as the lady awkwardly stood as well. I supposed she would walk by without looking at me, but then I realized I was guilty of misjudging her character.

I waited as she straightened her bent head, sniffled and slowly peered up at me. Her large dejected eyes were filled with a wonder I couldn't express in words. As an innocent tear dribbled down her ashen cheek, I was sure I could see a hint of a smile.

"Thank you," she whispered in a hushed tone. My throat tightened and tears threatened to fall down my cheeks.

"You're welcome," I murmured, offering a smile.

And you know what? She smiled then and a beautiful peacefulness washed over her once-stern countenance. I grinned widely as she cordially nodded her head and continued down the street, slowly creeping out of my life as quickly as she had appeared. Yet I knew that her smile and gratefulness would always be imprinted upon my life and heart.

When I finally had my frozen yogurt and my friend was still complaining about the embarrassment I had caused her, I felt gratitude well up within me. At that very moment, I didn't care anymore what other people thought. I was going to do the right thing, even if it meant losing or embarrassing my friends. I smiled to myself because even though I had helped that lady in such a small way, she had helped me more by showing me how I could be different in the world and how good that could feel.

Amy Hilborn

One Single Rose

It's not how much we give, but how much love we put into giving.

Mother Teresa

It was Valentine's Day, my freshman year of high school. I was so young, the romantic type, and I longed for a boyfriend or secret admirer. I walked the halls seeing couples holding hands, girls with huge smiles on their faces, and dozens of roses being delivered to "that special someone." All I wanted was a rose. A single rose to brighten up my Valentine's Day. But I was picky. I didn't want the rose from my parents, my sister or even my best friend. I wanted it from a secret admirer.

Valentine's Day at school was over, and I had no rose to hang in my locker like I had hoped. I came home a little sad and hoped next year's Valentine's Day would be better. I sat in my room dreaming about next year's romantic Valentine's Day when the doorbell rang. There at the front door was a deliveryman bringing one single rose to my house. Surely this rose wasn't for me. I didn't have such luck. I closed the front door with the rose in my hand and gave it to my mother. "Open the card!" she insisted when I told her it must be for her. I unsealed the envelope as my hands were shaking. Why were my hands shaking? I knew it wasn't for me. I slowly lifted the card and read what it said:

To Amanda

From someone who cares

I must have read it twenty times in a matter of seconds, praying my eyes weren't playing tricks on me. But they weren't. The rose was for me. I must have been happy for about five minutes, until I started calling the obvious people and accusing them of sending me a rose and playing a joke on my hopelessly romantic heart. No one knew who sent it to me. My friends, family and relatives were as surprised to hear I got a rose from a secret someone as much as I was. I was on cloud nine for weeks. Every time in high school that I felt down, I would think about my freshman year's Valentine's Day and a smile would appear.

Senior year rolled around and the dreaded February fourteenth was once again upon us. This year I received at least six carnations (a carnation-selling fundraiser was held at school that year), all from my best friends. I walked around with a big smile on my face, holding my flowers. Even though they were just from friends, they made me happy.

The end of the day was drawing to a close, and I had two classes left to show off my flowers. I walked into my French class and noticed one of my closest French class friends looking upset. I had grown to know my French classmates pretty well, since I had spent three of my high-school years with the same people in one class. We'd turned into a little French family. Well, my friend saw me walk in with my six flowers and lowered her head with tears in her eyes. She hadn't received a single flower, not even from her best friend.

We talked a few minutes before class, and some very familiar words came out of her mouth. "All I wanted was one single rose." My heart ached as I heard those words. The familiar sense of loneliness I had felt as a freshman, she was feeling now. I wanted to do something. It was too late to purchase carnations and I couldn't get her anything on a break because school was almost over. Finally, I figured it out. My freshman year. The single rose. That was it; that was what I had to do.

I told my mom about my plan and asked her if we could try to find a rose after our Valentine's dinner out. She remembered having seen a bucket of roses at a local drug store, so we rushed over and purchased the last good-looking rose and a small card. In order to preserve my identity, my mom wrote what I dictated to her in the card:

To Kristen
From someone who cares

We drove to her house trying to be discreet. I ran up to the front door, put the rose in her mailbox, rang the doorbell, ran back to the car and drove away. All the feelings of happiness I had felt my freshman year had all come flooding back. I just kept thinking that I was going to make someone feel as special as I had three years earlier.

The next day in school Kristen came up to me and gave me a hug with tears in her eyes. She had realized it was me by the handwriting. I guess my mom and I are more alike than I thought. She cried and said it was the nicest thing anyone had done for her in a while.

I never did figure out who it was who sent me that rose. But I did figure something else out. It didn't matter if it was a guy who secretly loved me, my mom trying to make me feel loved or an acquaintance who knew what I needed. What matters was that it was from someone who cared about me and who went out of their way to brighten up my day.

Amanda Bertrand

The Graduation Dance

A kind and compassionate act is often its own reward.

William John Bennett

I watched as my son walked purposefully toward the car with a look on his face that I knew so well. He was bursting to tell me some news about the eighth-grade graduation dance he'd just attended. As I waited in the parking lot with the windows open on that warm summer night, I had to smile. Adam had always been the type of kid to come home from school spurting out exciting or unhappy experiences about his day before the screen door had even slammed behind him.

"I did the best thing I ever did in my whole life tonight," he blurted out as soon as he put one foot in the car. The smile on his face spread from earlobe to earlobe. Pretty strong words for a person who's only been in existence for fourteen years.

The story spilled out of him like a hole in a bag of coffee beans.

"I was standing with Justin, Mark, Kristen and Britney,"

he began. "It was noisy and dark and everyone was dancing and laughing. Then Britney pointed out a girl to me
who was standing off into a darkened corner, kind of crying to herself.

"She told me, 'Go dance with her, Adam.'

"I told her she was crazy. First of all, I didn't even know
the girl. I mean, I've seen her around, but I didn't know
her name or anything. It's not like I'm friends with her or
anything.

"But then Britney started bugging me. She told me
how I have a responsibility to people because I was voted
Most Popular. She said I should be a role model, and that
I had the chance to do something special by dancing with
this girl. She said we're here to make a difference in other
people's lives, and if I danced with this girl, I'd make a
difference."

"Did you dance with her?" I asked him.

"No, Mom. I told Britney she was really crazy, because
she didn't even know why the girl was crying. That's
when she said something that really made me think. She
said, 'You know why she's crying, Adam. We both do.
Look at her. It's her eighth-grade graduation dance, and
she's standing alone in a corner. She's a little overweight,
and she's in a room full of teenagers who only care about
what kind of clothes they're wearing and what their hair
looks like. Think about it. How long did you spend trying
to decide what you were going to wear tonight? Well, she
did the same thing. Only no one is noticing, and no one
cares. Here's your chance to prove you deserve to be
voted Most Popular.'"

"So did you then?" I asked.

"No," he said. "I told Britney she was right, but that
everybody would laugh at me if I danced with her. So I told
Britney I didn't want to look weird and I wouldn't do it."

"What happened?" I asked.

"Well, Britney wouldn't stop bugging me. She told me that if people laughed at me because I danced with an unpopular girl, then they weren't people I needed to care about. Then she asked me if I saw any guy dancing with her, would I laugh? Or would I secretly have a lot of respect for that person?

"I knew she was right. But it was still hard to go over and ask her to dance. What if I walked all the way across the room in front of everyone and she turned me down? But Britney said, 'She won't turn you down, but even if she does, you'll get over it. I promise you, if you dance with her, she'll remember you for the rest of her life. This is your chance to make a difference.'

"So I went over to the girl and asked what her name was. Then I asked if she wanted to dance. She said yes and as we walked out to the dance floor, the music changed to a slow dance. I felt my face turn all red, but it was dark and I didn't think anyone noticed. I thought everyone was looking at me, but no one laughed or anything and we danced the whole dance.

"The weird thing is that Britney was right. It was three minutes out of my life, but it felt so good. And for the rest of the night, a lot of the guys danced with her and with anyone else they saw who hadn't danced yet. It was like the greatest eighth-grade graduation dance, because no one got left out. I really learned something tonight, Mom."

So did I, Adam, so did I.

Linda Chiara

Mary

I met my friend Mary when I was fifteen years old. Our friendship was different than most. Mary was ninety-three years old when I met her. Almost a century separated us.

Mary's family lived far away, and they considered sending her to a nursing home so she could receive proper care. She, however, desperately wanted to stay in her own little home. My best friend's mother was visiting Mary one day and suggested that someone come into her house to take care of her. Mary asked her if she knew anybody who would be interested and my friend's mother told her I might be. I had been looking for a little extra cash.

A couple of days later, my mom and I went over to Mary's to get acquainted. I got the job and we shook hands. After that I came to her house every evening at 6:00 P.M.

Our nightly ritual consisted of:

Her telling me about her day.

Me telling her about mine.

Her telling me what she wanted fixed for dinner (every detail).

Me fixing dinner.

Me serving her dinner, filling up her water glass and getting her pills.

Watching *Wheel of Fortune*.

Then, watching *My Three Sons* or *Leave It to Beaver* (I think I've seen every episode by now).

Me washing the dishes.

Me sometimes taking out the garbage or washing clothes.

Me shaking her hand (it became our little ritual) and leaving.

This filled up a couple of hours each night. I already had a busy schedule, so my mom would help out and take care of Mary some evenings.

Going to Mary's gave me some relief from the pressure-filled world of adolescence. Just being with her gave me a mental rest from my busy life. Also, she was a kindred spirit. She never got angry at me when I boiled the potato instead of baked it, or when I (constantly) set off the fire alarm due to baking challenges. She would tell me stories, and of course she had many. She talked to me about her late husband and her children growing up on their old farm. She knew about everything. Well, she had ninety-three years of experience. She showed me pictures and told me what it used to be like when she was a teenager in the early 1900s. I told her about the changing world and what it was like for me to be a teenager.

About a year and a half later she got sick and had to go to the hospital for a couple of days. The next thing I knew, she had died. It was a shock. Many people in my life have died, but Mary had become such an everyday part of my life. At her funeral, Mary's daughter thanked all of us who had made it possible for her to stay in her home for the last year of her life. I was thankful that I could be a helping hand. But when I thought about it more, I realized that Mary had helped *me*. She taught me lessons that school could never teach, and her house was a sanctuary for me during some hard times.

I slipped inside the house to say my good-byes. First, to her family, and then to her. The living room was completely empty, but it still had that indescribable smell. I could picture her in her armchair, smiling. I whispered my good-bye.

Mary was my friend. She didn't care if my hair was messy or if my clothes were not name-brand. I could even go to her house in my PJs. I could be me. And that's the greatest gift a friend can give.

Jodi Rudin

May I Help You?

Something that has always puzzled me all my life is why, when I am in special need of help, the good deed is usually done by somebody on whom I have no claim.

William Feather

We stood in the street and cried. Not great, heaving sobs, but the slow, sweaty tears of desperation. We were eighteen and crying, alone on a sidewalk only hours after arriving in Honduras, Central America. We were there to join a development project called Project Bayan as volunteers, but apparently we had the wrong number for the project headquarters because we were unable to make contact.

The massive humidity was piggybacked by an intense heat that parched our throats. Where would we find purified water in the steaming jungles of Honduras? Our vocal chords were strangled by an inability to speak Spanish. It was all we could do to stand in the street and cry.

To our left was a jumble of automotive confusion, and to our right was an open-air bakery. We didn't notice the table of Spanish speakers commenting on our obvious plight until a man approached us.

"Hello," he said, in perfect English.

Our tear-streaked faces stared at this unexpected friendliness.

"My name is Henry Wilkins," he continued. "I don't like to see people crying in my country. May I help you?"

It was three simple sentences. But it was all we needed. We poured out our dilemma. We were lost; we were exhausted; we were hungry; and we were thirsty. We didn't know what was safe to eat or drink, and we didn't know how to get in touch with people who seemed to exist on the other side of an inaccessible language barrier. Neither one of us, accustomed to the security of family and friends, had ever felt so alone.

And somehow, Henry Wilkins, a man who'd grown up oppressed because of the color of his skin, poverty-stricken because of the state of his country's economy, and without stability because of the corruption of his government, took us to the supermarket and found us food. Then he took us to the café and found us water. Henry Wilkins took us to the phone and found our friends. And Henry Wilkins did this because he didn't like to see people crying in his country.

I have been home from Honduras for over two years now, but I still think often of Henry Wilkins. I remain convinced that Henry Wilkins was an angel. I also remain convinced that Henry Wilkins taught me one of the most valuable lessons of friendship I learned during my entire, life-changing stay in Honduras. It was three simple sentences that are etched into my heart and that I intend to keep with me the rest of my life: "My name is Bobbi Smith. I don't like to see people crying in my country. May I help you?"

Bobbi Smith

7

GROWING UP

There came a time when the risk to remain tight in a bud was more painful than the risk it took to blossom.

Anaïs Nin

The Need for Speed

Nobody told me what to expect during my teenage years. But what I was most unprepared for was loss. Not just loss of childhood, but loss of innocence and simplicity, too. I felt like I was standing between two continents, childhood and adulthood, in some in-between, nowhere zone.

So I started doing crazy things that involved speed. Like clinging to the roof of a car while my buddy T. J. gunned the engine and spun in circles in an empty parking lot at night—knowing full well if I were to slip or let go, my life would be over. Or like skiing or biking down steep hills so fast I could barely stay in control—all without a helmet. Was it that the speed made me feel alive? Or was I trying to get away from everything around me?

Although by all accounts I was a normal, soccer-playing, sixteen-year-old suburban kid on the north shore of Chicago, with a B-plus average, a doctor for a father and a housewife for a mother, everything seemed to be going haywire around me. I started losing friends in dramatic ways, one after another.

First there was my friend Nick, the basketball team captain, the football quarterback, the guy every guy wanted to be and every girl had a crush on. One sunny suburban day, Nick crashed his motorcycle into a truck. The next day he was paralyzed from the waist down for life. *For life?* I couldn't fathom the notion. I tried to stay friends with him, but the Nick I knew was gone.

Next was John, the lead guitarist in the coolest band, the guy who would shut his eyes on stage, lean back, bathed in a magenta glow, and let his fingers scatter up the frets, effortlessly, while everyone gawked. He got heavy into drugs, invited his girlfriends to climb the tree outside his window to his bedroom where they'd have sex, and then he'd help them down the tree before dawn. Very Romeo and Juliet, he thought. I'd been friends with John forever and knew that there was something basically good in him that had gotten buried. But whenever I saw him his eyes were glazed over and he could barely walk, and I soon realized there was nothing left between us. He tried suicide a few times in a few different ways, and one frigid January Sunday, his parents had the men in white take him, yelling and screaming, to a psychiatric clinic.

Then my friend Heather, who had always been a great student, suddenly became obsessed over perfecting her homework. She wrote and rewrote term papers, staying up all night, going to sleep just before dawn, walking zombielike through school corridors, lost, often bewildered, always postponing handing in papers so she could make changes. In class, she began plucking hairs from the crown of her head. Her parents sent her away, too.

Those were the dramatic losses. But I felt everyone was pulling away, growing faster, doing more, knowing more, being smarter, moving quicker, getting more grades, girls, glamour. I couldn't get a handle on it. And nobody seemed to be paying any attention to those of us who were left behind.

One day, T. J. asked me to go winter camping about two

hours north in Wisconsin. He had the whole thing figured out: We'd snowshoe in with backpacks, a gas stove, sleeping bags and a tent. We'd stay a weekend, then miss a day of school. That was the part that intrigued me: It was a statement to everyone at school that I was different, not interested in the usual stuff, the kind of guy who could take care of himself. "What if there's a freak storm and we freeze?" I asked. He looked at me as if to say, *Danger is what we're after, right?* Against all odds, my parents, after hours of haggling, let me go with him.

So there I was, leaning against the hood of T. J.'s car, strapping on snowshoes. "I never used these," I said. "Just like walking," he replied. But it wasn't. For me, it was more like floating—above the world, above my worries. I liked the slow pace, the tracks I left behind me and the untouched snow ahead.

It wasn't that night, when we made a partial igloo, pitched our tent, melted snow to make water, cooked a pathetic astronautlike meal and fell into deep sleep. Nor was it on the second day, when we melted more snow and fretted about the need for water and the threat of dehydration. But on our last day, it warmed by ten degrees and everything around us started to melt. T. J. was going on about new dangerous stuff we could do back home: laying down on streets so startled drivers would have to stop; climbing up roofs of cheerleaders' houses and tapping on their windows; throwing iceballs at cars as they drove down a lonely ravine, hoping the drivers might chase us . . . when he spotted an iced-over pond and dared me to touch the center. A voice said, *No.* The more he urged me on, the more I had to get away. I began to snowshoe up a ridge, and then I continued until there was no sign of T. J., where the only sounds were my breath and snow falling in clumps off pines.

Suddenly, inexplicably, a surge of sadness seemed to

pulse through my feet, up my legs, through my arms and right out my skull. It wasn't like crying, more like an eruption . . . and it felt good, natural, sane. And when it ceased, some time later, I realized it was just me in the world, but that was a gift, not a curse. My life was mine to make or break. It was my show, my ball game. I couldn't control everything. But I realized I'd lost more than just friends: I'd temporarily lost myself. The speed I'd been seeking by clinging to the top of cars in parking lots hadn't helped me find myself. One-step-at-a-time snowshoes had.

James D. Barron

On Shame and Shadowboxing

*Nothing is so strong as gentleness, and nothing
is so gentle as real strength.*

Ralph W. Sockman

That summer I spent my days with a group of young
men whose long, stringy hair was bleached from sun and
saltwater. This was in Corpus Christi, Texas, on the Gulf
Coast, and the boys went surfing in the mornings then
returned in the afternoons to play football on my parents'
lawn. My parents warned me about them. They knew
about cars and smoked cigarettes, and when they took off
their shirts for our games, their chests and arms were
hard with muscle that came from paddling out into the
ocean before dawn. Girls fawned over them, and that
summer I idolized them, too. I've forgotten all but one of
their names, Barry, though maybe another was called
Todd. Always in this ever-present gang of boys there is
one named Todd.

My father didn't like the boys smoking around me or
their long hair, and he didn't like things he'd heard about
them, things he wouldn't tell me. But he wanted me to

spend more time outside and must have figured that since the games took place in our front yard, the shadow of our house would protect me from them, from their influence.

Earlier that year my father had taught me to throw a football, and by summer I could pass the length of two, sometimes three, lawns. These were high, arching throws that should not have come from the small arms of a boy who preferred books to ball games. Every time I heaved the football, I expected it to veer off course into a window or under the tire of a passing car, but instead it almost always went where I wanted it to, into that pocket of my father's chest and arms. "Perfect," he would say. "Right in the numbers." When I played football with the boys, I was "All-Time Quarterback," which meant that I threw for both teams and got sacked a lot.

In addition to teaching me how to throw long bombs, my father also taught me how to fight. He stressed that I should never throw the first punch, but once it's thrown, I shouldn't hold back. My father had fought a lot: In his youth, in the army and once in a pool hall after a man made a vulgar innuendo toward my mother. He taught me how to shadowbox and how to hit someone, how to twist my fist just as it made impact so that it cut the skin. He encouraged me to bite, scratch and pull hair, to use sticks or attack from behind, to kick whoever had started the fight in the shins or between the legs, or to stomp the bridges of his feet. I nodded as my father told me these things, but I knew if the time came, I would worry that hitting someone would only make him hurt me worse. In the pool hall, my father had hit the man in the knee with a pool cue, and when I asked him if it had broken, he said, "The stick or his leg?"

Maybe I wanted so badly for Barry and Todd and the boys to accept me because each of them seemed more like the young man my father was than I did. And maybe, too, that's why my father worried about my time with them and taught me how to fight. He thought the boys would bully me, take advantage of my adoration, and he knew I would not snitch on them. I would suffer their insults and mockery because I feared bringing trouble to anyone, and he saw that these boys thrived on trouble, as probably he had.

But in the summer when I was fourteen, the boys tolerated me because of my quarterback abilities and my parents' long, even lawn. The target of their harassment that summer was a boy named Robert, but they called him Roberta. They called him Roberta because of a high voice and the feminine lightness in his stride, something like a prance. For three months, he stayed with his grandmother who lived across the street from my family. Robert usually left on his bicycle in the mornings and returned in the afternoons while we played football. When he rode past, the boys acted as if they were going to peg him with the football. Although they never actually threw it, every time one of them dropped back and took aim with the ball, Robert flinched. Sometimes he fell off the bicycle and turned red. If his grandmother tottered outside, the boys waved at her and asked Robert if he wanted to join the game. He never did.

I felt sorry for him and hated to see him turn the corner on his bicycle because I knew Barry and Todd would start insulting him. He made an easy target, and for all of their muscle and mouthing off, for all of their bragging and bravado, they were weak, insecure boys. But I never interfered with their cruel impressions of his prance or tried to silence the jokes they made about his voice; I just waited for the game to resume. As much as I wanted them to lay off of Robert, there was always the great sense of relief that the insults weren't being hurled at me.

After almost an entire summer of enduring their threats and slurs, something happened on a hot August afternoon. I'm not sure what changed that day; maybe they'd finally pushed him too far, or maybe he'd been planning it all summer. Maybe he'd been scouting our games like a coach from an opposing team, looking for weaknesses, trying to identify the player who would fumble or fall most easily. When Barry and Todd started in on Robert when he returned from his bike ride, he didn't retreat. Instead of sulking away, he stood flat-footed in his grandmother's driveway and started insulting me. I can still hear his high, girly voice coming across the street, across all of these years.

I hoped the boys would rush to my defense, but as Robert marched into my yard, they only laughed, their eyes boring into me as if it were the showdown they'd been waiting for all along. My knees trembled as they did when I had to speak with girls. With everything Robert said, the boys cackled louder. He fed off their laughter, his words growing louder and more harsh, and soon the boys rallied behind him and egged him on. They listened to him as a football team listens to its quarterback.

That afternoon when he gathered the courage and confidence to insult me, I did the one thing that would have disappointed my father: I threw the first punch. I whipped a hard, perfect spiral into Robert's face. Then as he brought up his hands, I exploded across the yard like a fullback charging for a touchdown, barreled into his chest and knocked him to the ground. The boys closed in around us, yelling and laughing. Robert and I grappled with each other—he was much stronger than I would have anticipated—then I managed to mount and straddle his chest. Aside from an awkward, frantic slap that bloodied my nose, I owned the fight. My fists flurried on his face, and his pale, freckled flesh tore between my knuckles and his cheekbones.

Soon my father broke through the boys around us and pulled me off him. Because he never learned the truth behind the fight—Robert, like me, would never tell—I knew he was proud of me. I felt ashamed, and even then wished I had the strength to walk into my house and leave the boys in the sun. The truth is, while I've grown to resemble my father in many ways—his stubborn optimism, his broad, round shoulders and his inclination to protect those he loves—on that day in the yard, I was the weak one. I think Robert understood this. He saw me as an outsider in the group, someone like himself who would never quite fit in, and he knew the boys would turn on me. If his eyes would have been open, he would have seen that I winced with each strike, and was as scared and ashamed and in as much pain as he was. It was as if I were shadowboxing, throwing blows at my own image, and with each swing, I came that much closer to connecting.

Bret Anthony Johnston

Spare Change

Life has no limitations except the ones you make.

Les Brown

I'm seated in the back row of Mrs. Andrew's sixth-grade class. I wriggle tightly in the stiff-backed, wooden desk/ chair combination, which is unfairly constructed for a right-handed world. I hold my pencil firmly in my left hand and try to conform to the ill-fitting desk. I'm not just different because of my anti-dexterity; there are many things that make me peculiar to the world.

First of all, there are my clothes. My dad's blue-collar salary limits my fashion ability. No penny is spent frivolously. In my family's nightly ritual, Dad hauls down the four-liter jug from the shelf over the kitchen sink. Into the glass he empties both pockets. Pennies, dimes and nickels sing out the tinkle of a poor man's wallet. We are a family of coin rollers. My mom's purse is not filled with singles or tens; it is weighted down by rolls of change, as though she were ready at a moment's notice to hit the Vegas slot machines. Oh, how carefree it must feel to line your pockets with paper currency as unencumbered as air.

You would think by looking at my clothes that we're back in 1975. My mom uses words like "retro" to try and convince me that my clothes are cool. Kids at my school shop at thrift stores for cool vintage T-shirts; they buy their jeans at the Gap. But not me. I'm branded with the wardrobe of a victim. It's like wearing a neon sign that reads: All future psychotics take out frustrations and misplaced anger right here! As you will find in most schools, there is that one classification of child—the bully—who immediately reads the signs and moves in for the kill. Many adults claim that the bully is himself a "victim" of his own self-hatred. However, all this means little to those of us who have been subjected to the bully's misunderstood and misspent anger.

While in class, it is my sole intention to innocently blend in with the herd—little chance of that. Carefully, I press my pencil against the workbook page. The numbers blur into one huge, fuzzy black caterpillar. My mind is a thousand miles away from these division problems. Instead, I'm thinking about my pencil—of all things. I'm trying to write with it ever so lightly, so I don't snap the point. A visit to the pencil sharpener would mean a certain run-in with my bully, who conveniently sits alongside it and the exit door. It is only a matter of time before my lead or my bladder give out.

Then comes the moment when I am forced to visit the sharpener. My pencil in one hand, I begin turning the crank. I don't get very far before his hand reaches out and grabs my arm, spinning me round roughly to face him.

"Going somewhere, Dog Face?"

I try to answer him, but all that issues from my mouth is a tightly choked whisper, "No."

As if strengthened by my weakness, his laughter becomes the public-address system that calls the others. "Where'd you get that bird's nest you call hair—the

circus?" he asks, pointing to my huge sprouts of long
frizzy tendrils. Each wiry brown strand defies entrapment
by any elastic scrunchee. "Did you stick your hand in an
electric socket, Dog Face?" His comments raise not only
the pitch of laughter around the room, but the pressure I
feel building behind my eyes. Finally, like an engorged
geyser, tears burst forth and the bully's victory is assured.

Tears are the blood that bullies savor. They're proof of
dominance among the herd. It's hard to explain how
deeply he can hurt me with his simple words. It's a pain
that can choke my windpipes and strangle my heart. He
tells me I'm ugly, and inside I agree. Is it possible I hate
myself for crying more than I hate him?

I run away from my bully and the laughter, and head
for the girls' bathroom. Inside these walls I still believe it's
possible to wash away all suffering and tears. While water
may wash away most tear-stained traces, it can never
bathe the anguish that grips so tightly at my heart.

But all this happened to me many years ago, when I was
a younger and different person. Now, I'm seventeen and
headed for college. In the years since, my dad got a new job,
and we moved to another town. I have not seen my bully in
over five years, and there have been no other bullies to take
his place. I have grown not only outside, but inside as well.
In my new school I've made friends who accept me, and
I've grown not only to accept, but even like myself. Though
times are better for us financially, my dad still keeps that jug
filled with change—just in case. I'm no longer ashamed of
my family. Instead, with maturity, I have learned to respect
their strength and tenacity.

Now I am standing in line waiting to sign up for classes
for my first semester of college. The room is packed with
others like me, nervously anticipating what lies ahead:
meeting new people, trying a new life on for size.
Suddenly, I notice my bully standing in a corner of the

room looking as puzzled and threatened as anyone else—but he doesn't see me. I panic at the sight of him. I recognize the slant of his smile and the furl of his brow. He can still set ripples of acid swirling through my belly.

I can't believe he's going to the same school as me. In that short moment, two scenarios run through my mind: I can run over, slap him in the face, shake him and demand to know why he made my life a living hell. But what would happen if I run over and slap him, and then he slaps me back and we both end up getting hauled away by campus security?

This is what really happened: I looked over at him, and then I looked over at the long line for names A to H, and that's when it hit me. Why waste my time living in the past? That bully *was* my history, and now it was time to turn toward my future. I couldn't move ahead until I came to terms with that simple concept. So I got in line and registered, and then I got in the next line, and the next, and the next. This bully meant nothing to my present life or dreams. There was nothing I needed to say to him anymore, because he no longer meant anything to me. He appeared so much smaller to me now. With this realization, my mind's eye shrank him down further, until there was nothing left of him that mattered now at all.

That day I let go of my bully who, I thought, held power over me for so long, and all it took was a conscious decision to do so. It wasn't the bully who kept me prisoner—it was my own spirit. I realized that I must live each day in the present, and not allow myself to sink into the murkiness of a lost childhood. Each day is like a brand-new penny, which I value and spend wisely. At night I toss them inside a kind of glass jug in my mind. As they hit bottom they resonate with the splendid tinkling of a life filled with possibilities.

Alyssa Morgan
As told to C. S. Dweck

The Rumor Was True

I do not think much of a man who is not wiser today than he was yesterday.

Abraham Lincoln

Junior-high school was probably the worst time in my life. My body was changing daily, and I spent most of my time trying to fit into a mold that my peers had formed for me. Gone were the days of Elmer's glue, crayons and those tiny scissors with the rounded edges. From here on out, I had my own locker, carried my books to each class and started making my own decisions about which classes to take. Oh yeah, I almost forgot: I had to take showers in front of my peers. Naked. That was dreadful.

What I remember most about junior high, however, was the incredible pain and heartache that students inflicted on one another with their words and actions. There were students who seemed to have it all together and made those around them feel as if they didn't measure up. It wasn't until much later that I learned that those who ripped on others suffered from a terrible self-image, so in order to make themselves feel better, they tore others down. In fact, they were usually a totally different person from the one they presented to the outside world.

I didn't have the best self-image in junior high, and there were two things that I fell back on to be accepted—athletics and humor. I have always been a decent athlete, which brought a certain confidence to my life, and I have always been able to make people laugh. At times, the laughter came at another's expense.

I didn't fully realize what I was doing to the self-images of those around me, particularly one classmate of mine. Her name was Tracy, and she had a crush on me. Instead of nicely letting her know that I wasn't interested in her, I got caught up in trying to be funny, with her being the brunt of my jokes. I am ashamed now to think of how I treated her in seventh grade. I went out of my way to make things miserable for her. I made up songs about her, and even wrote short stories in which I had to save the world from Tracy, the evil villain.

That all changed about halfway through the year, however, when Mr. Greer, my PE teacher, came up to me one day.

"Hey, Mike, you got a second?"

"Sure, Mr. Greer!" I said. Everybody loved Mr. Greer, and I looked up to him like a father.

"Mike, I heard a rumor that you were going around picking on Tracy." He paused and looked me straight in the eye. It seemed like an eternity before he continued.

"You know what I told the person I heard that from? I told them it couldn't possibly be true. The Mike Powers I know would never treat another person like that. Especially a young lady."

I gulped, but said nothing. He gently put his hand on my shoulder and said, "I just thought you should know that." Then he turned and walked away without a backward glance, leaving me to my thoughts.

That very day I stopped picking on Tracy. I knew that the rumor was true, and that I had let my role model down by my actions. More importantly, though, it made me realize how badly I must have hurt this girl and others for whom I had made life difficult. It was probably a couple of months later before I fully realized the incredible way in which Mr. Greer handled the problem. He not only made me realize the seriousness of my actions, but he did it in a way that helped me to save some of my pride. My respect and love for him grew even stronger after that.

I don't think I ever apologized to Tracy for my hurtful words and actions. She moved away the next year, and I never saw her again. While I was very immature as a seventh-grader, I still should have known better. In fact, I did know better, but it took the wisdom of my favorite teacher to bring it out into the light.

Michael T. Powers

Stupidity

*Keep true, never be ashamed of doing right;
decide on what you think is right and stick to it.*

George Eliot

He looked full-grown compared to the other children,
and his arms and hands were constantly moving, as if he
had no control over them. He talked curiously, in a language my second-grade ears could not decipher. He
laughed like the rest of us, though perhaps a little louder
and sometimes when there was nothing to laugh about.
Other children called him "slow" and "retarded" and
"stupid"—words I was only beginning to understand, and
that made me uncomfortable, like toes trapped in shoes
that are too small.

I have a stark memory of him that took place during the
innocent time of day every student longed for, when the
bell rang and herds of children stampeded out the door of
the large, brick building called Central School and scattered like sheep on the playground to expend excess
energy on swings or monkey bars, teeter-totters or sand-
boxes. I chose the swings that day, for I liked the way the

wind lifted my hair like an opening umbrella, cooling my face and neck on my way up to the treetops, where I challenged myself to swing high enough to kick the leaves on the branches.

From my vantage point, I observed a large crowd of children gathering around the "stupid" boy, holding hands as they orbited around him, chanting something I could not make out from a distance.

Something about the scene was bothersome to me, and I jumped from the swing still in motion, stumbling to my knees in my haste to get to the scene in question. As I neared the crowd, I could see the large, clumsy boy in the center of the whirling children, laughing, drool spilling from his chin, his arms flopping up and down as he pranced on his tiptoes. The group was chanting "Gravy Train, Gravy Train." Someone invited me to join in the "fun," but the display paralyzed me as I looked on through eyes suddenly blurred by tears. The "retarded" boy didn't have the capacity to realize he was being made fun of, thinking instead that he was taking part in a game, making the taste of salty tears in my mouth all the more repulsive.

I silently vowed that day never to take part in making fun of others because they were "different."

I have seen the boy repeatedly over the years in the bodies of many people with cruel labels attached to their names—the brunts of hurtful jokes, the misfits, the nerds, the deformed, the shy, the helpless, the ugly, the friendless—and I have also experienced the humiliation of being the lonely one inside the circle of chanting "children."

I wish I could say I remained true to my vow and boast complete innocence to indifference and bigotry, but I have done my share of gossiping in the cafeteria behind the back of one who could not even defend herself. I have laughed at demeaning jokes and scoffed at someone's choice of clothing. I even feared for my safety because of the color of someone's skin. But more often than not, I quickly regretted it, haunted by the memory of a retarded boy, alone inside a moving circle of taunting children chanting "Gravy Train," and I am the one too "stupid" to not laugh.

Marjee Berry-Wellman

Waves of Good-Bye

In the highway breeze, Adie's hair whips her cheeks like a dozen inky horsetails. Most of her mane has fallen out of her upsweep, the strands flapping wildly around her face, around her exposed shoulders. Alongside our Jeep, the beach yawns, waking with its seagulls and surfers. Adie turns up the radio, and we belt out the chorus in our best high notes until our voices drown into the ocean air. It is senior ditch day, after all, and we have much rejoicing to do.

We were both Leos, and our manes, we reasoned, were direct extensions of ourselves. It sounded very sensible, even a little mystical, lending justification to our nicknames at high school: the two good witches. Adie and I would do everything imaginable to our locks: curling, straightening, knotting, weaving, teasing. Adie's hair was so much more alive with possibility: Her black hair cascaded lazily from her scalp, and when the sunlight hit it just right, it had a way of reflecting silvery pools in its loose waves. My hair, a kind of dusty orange, had an unmanageable thickness about it, a dull frumpiness that took a backseat to Adie's slicker twists and braids.

With her foot still planted on the gas pedal, Adie manages to stand up in the Jeep. Her head is peering over the windshield, high above the roll bars. Even in her rashness, she is graceful—a statuesque performer balancing upon the spine of a Lippizan.

"Adie!" I holler. "You're insane! Get down!"

"Come on and live a little," she sing-songs. "We're nearly done with high school! Can you believe it? I mean, can you beee-lieve it?"

Adie collapses back to the seat, exhilarated with her feat. She mutters something about trig class, only I am far away now. I glance to the seamless shore and think, for the first time, about *after* high school, and everything becomes the hollow sucking sound of the sea in a conch. Come fall, Adie will be at a university in San Diego, and I will be navigating my way around a campus in Santa Barbara. One shore, two separate cities, an entire world away.

Her hands come off the steering wheel and reach toward the sky in an utterly free stretch. My hands are suddenly curling nervously around my kneecaps.

We have our usual spot, between lifeguard stands 11 and 12, which we have methodically stalked out over four years, finding it to be the spot for the best-looking lifeguards. Our towels are unfurled, the radio antenna elongated, and the baby oil is at the ready.

"Adie?" I ask. She is dousing herself in oil, which gives her a ubiquitous sheen. "Have you thought about what college will be like?"

"Mmmmm, not really," she answers. The question seems to slide off her back like the oil itself. "I guess I'll just find out when it happens."

"Right, right," I say, half-assuredly. "That's how I feel." Only I don't. Horrific images of wandering, lost, in a sea of people—mature people with bills and rent—streak across my mind. I worry about the notorious bike paths I was warned of at orientation, about devilish seniors careening and forcing me off the road, and about who my roommate will be, and if she'll have lousy taste in music. "Isn't it funny how we know all of the same words to the same songs?" I ask.

"What? Are you day dreaming again?" Adie replies. "Here," she continues, handing me the baby oil, "can you coat my back?" With the sun striking her, she already appears perfectly bronze, a stark contrast to my pale skin mottled with freckles.

She is lying with her belly to the sun and a towel over her face. "You know," she says, removing the towel for a moment, "I bet you'll be the only one in your dorm with red hair."

As if I weren't self-conscious enough! No amount of good-witchery could mask the peculiarity of my hair.

"You're lucky," she continues. "It's what makes you, you," and the towel goes back over her eyes.

"I think it's time to flip," Adie announces. We roll over, repositioning ourselves perpendicular to the sun, when a deep voice overhead startles us.

"Hi ladies. Hard day at the office?" He is tall, almost unbearably tan, and his hair falls over one eye.

"The hardest," Adie responds, propping herself up on one arm. She usually takes the lead in these things, while I wait to chime in. Sometimes I wait eternities.

His hands are on his hips now, angling his torso and flashing ripples of muscle. I think about how I look. Should I lean on one arm? Is my stomach in? Am I showing cleavage? Do I even have cleavage? Adie seems to be doing everything right. Her body is relaxed and firm at once. I seem light-years behind. "Well," he says, "I'm headed out to catch some waves," and he heads toward the breakers.

"Now this," Adie mumbles, "is how I imagine college."

And then he turns around, looking straight at me. "You coming or what?"

Steve. It's an older name. A real guy name. The water is up to our chests, lapping haphazardly at our throats. When the sun hits, it blinds us temporarily, and then we laugh, trying to keep our balance in the ocean.

"So I take it you don't work," Steve questions. "How about school?"

I nod. This is uncharted territory.

"UCLA?" he asks. "No, wait, you look like a Pepperdine girl."

My nodding gets wilder.

"Which one?"

"Ummm. Neither."

"Oh, a private school, then."

Our high school *is* private, I reason, agreeing with him. And then his hands are about my waist.

"Watch this," he whispers, and then tosses me up out of the ocean, and I crash back in through the water, submerged with a deep sloshing of water. I force my way back up to the surface, gasping. "Pretty good," Steve boasts, only I have no idea about what's so good about any of this.

My eyes rove the shore and I see Adie there, and she sees me, giving an exaggerated wave. Maybe this *is* like college, I think, my being on my own—floating—and Adie somewhere further off, wondering where I've gone. It has always been me waving back at Adie, watching her flirt, wondering when she will come back to land, or if she will. Now, I am my own element of surprise. I wave back to her, just barely, unassuredly, holding up my hand like a hesitant bicyclist unsure of the proper signal.

"You seem close to your friend," Steve inquires. "Same school?"

Yes, I answer, but not for long. When I finally tell him that we are just two girls, two seniors, ditching school, he isn't as repulsed as I feared. In fact, he becomes a little too anxious to give advice about college, about the freedoms and the friendships, about the failing and forgetting, all of the "f's." "It comes in waves," he says, and then, smiling, he splashes water into my face. "Get it?"

This time I nod genuinely, I get it, and, with my body chilled from the coolness of the ocean or maybe just from the coolness of everything, head back toward the shore where my best friend is soaking in the sun, soaking in everything, still waving to me as I wander back to her.

Jennifer Baxton

When It All Changes

The moment of change is the only poem.

Adrienne Rich

I am reminded of the song we used to sing in Girl Scouts: "Make new friends, but keep the old; one is silver and the other's gold." I graduated from high school a year and a half ago, and post-graduation, the old seemed more like gold dust—it all just blew away. My friends and I went our separate ways and made different lives with people in our new worlds. I put away my old photos and shot new ones to go with my new furniture in my new apartment—in my new life. Once in a while I would call a friend at college or an ex back home and rehash the past. The conversation usually didn't exceed ten minutes because we didn't really know what to say to each other. Everything had changed.

I believe that in life we have chapters—phases, if you will. The many faces of youth are shocking. We change from day to day, hour to hour. We love and then stop. We have a best friend and then we have five. We love our parents and then hate them. We play soccer and then decide to take dance classes instead. Okay, so we're fickle—fickle like the latest fashion trend. "In with the new, out with the old," that's our motto. This way we never get bored and it's easier to move on after being hurt. The flip side is that there will be a point when we look back on the old and miss it, like we miss a pet that dies or a small house that isn't big enough for a growing family. Moving away from something is exciting, but it all looks different in the rearview mirror. While visiting my parents during Thanksgiving, I awoke to the backward mirror image of my forward life.

I called several of my high-school friends and suggested that we go out for coffee to catch up. Everyone agreed, and so we met downtown at a familiar café. We all looked a bit different—older, taller, thicker. We sipped our coffee drinks and chatted, talking mostly about high school, boyfriends and finals. We laughed and hugged and remembered. For some reason; talking and remembering made me feel pretty bad, and when there was nothing left to talk about, I realized that we hadn't really talked about anything. So much had happened in the last year with all of us that we couldn't possibly know where to start. I went home that night feeling really alone and confused, and frustrated with myself for . . . for what? Changing, I guess.

It took me about an hour to realize how ridiculous that sounded. I was feeling guilty for changing? I was confused because we had all endured another year and mastered new experiences. My guilt was short-lived. Sure, everything has changed because we have changed and will continue to change forever. We all care a little less about who wore what to the *MTV Awards* and what the latest toy trend is. (What's that scooter thing called again?) We have healed our hearts from the devastation of breaking up with our first loves. We are secure with the fact that no

matter what happens, we will always have tomorrow. We
have all changed in college, or in the University of Life.
Some of us have jobs, and some of us have boyfriends.
Next year, we will all have grown a little more, and then a
little more the next year. We will have pain, and we will
have joy. We will endure and we will accept, and then we'll
be back to share or just to smile with each other and know
that everything will be all right.

Rebecca Woolf

What's on the Inside

To measure the man, measure his heart.

Malcolm Stevenson Forbes

I can still remember that boy in perfect detail. He had beautiful blue eyes that lit up whenever he smiled. And when his mouth smiled, half of his face would light up with shiny white teeth. He was the first boy who gave me that feeling like my heart was going to stop. When he walked by, I could see him out of the corner of my eye and smell the detergent he used on his clothes. My body would freeze, and my brain would stop ticking. Then he would flash that big smile at me and my breath would stop. I can picture myself standing in front of him like a fool with my mouth gaping open and my eyes melting with lust as this beautiful boy charmed me.

There was no doubt about it, I was head-over-heels, madly in puppy love. I might have only been in third grade, but this was real or at least I thought it was. I was constantly thinking about him and ways I could get closer to him. "Eric" was scribbled all over my notebooks with messy little hearts drawn around them. I adored him, and he knew it.

Then one Saturday I got the chance to get closer to him. I was at a birthday party, and Eric showed up at the front door. The whole night I avoided him for fear that I would say something stupid.

As I was pigging out on potato chips, I turned around and saw him staring right at me. My stomach jumped and my cheeks blushed as he walked closer to me. He flashed his eyes at me and said, "Come here, Eleanor. I want to tell you something." My heart fluttered at the thought of being so close to him. Eric leaned closer and cupped his hand around my ear. He brought his face closer to mine, closer, closer. I moved my head away to give him more room, but he moved closer still. I felt his arm across my back and his hand warming my ear. But I didn't hear any words. I tilted my head away from him in an almost uncomfortable position and again his face moved closer to mine. I turned to look at him and there was his face, two inches from mine, with his eyes closed and his mouth pursed into a kiss. A wave of shock came over my face, and his expression copied mine as he opened his eyes.

"What are you doing?" he asked. He raised his eyebrows in a puzzled expression

"What are YOU doing?" I shot back. I could only imagine what Eric was thinking right now. I'm sure he was thinking, *This girl, Eleanor, is a dork!* I desperately hoped that wasn't what he was thinking.

He looked right at me and yelled, "Geez, Eleanor, I'm just trying to kiss you!"

What? He was going to kiss me? I missed my chance! My one and only chance to kiss this boy of my dreams, and I ruined it.

"Oh, sorry," I said, very embarrassed.

He gave me a small kiss on the cheek then scrambled off to a group of boys who were laughing hysterically.

Then he yelled at his friends. "I'm NEVER playing Truth-or-Dare again!"

At the sound of his words, my sensitive heart crumbled into pieces. *Tell me he didn't say what I thought he said.* But I knew it was true. I could feel a sob starting in the back of my throat, but I promised myself to hold it in. Then tears came, filling up my eyes and spilling over my bottom lashes. My lip started to quiver, and I knew a flood of tears was only seconds away. I flew out of the basement with my head in my hands and retreated to the bathroom to cry alone for the rest of the night.

As much as I would like to, I can't say that this experience was easily forgotten. That night, I realized Eric didn't like me as much as I liked him. The next week at school, I would hear groups of kids talking about the incident when they didn't think I was listening. But I heard them and my feelings were hurt each and every time. While my heart ached for a while, I actually recovered rather quickly. I got over it in a couple of weeks, and the gossip stopped long before that. I did learn a lesson, though, and it still helps me to this day. *There are a lot of cute boys out there, some even cuter than Eric, but just because a boy is cute doesn't mean he is necessarily nice.* I still get crushes on boys who are cute, but I find out what their personality is like before I let my heart get involved.

Eleanor Luken

And Still I Search . . .

Ah yes, it's all going to pay off, I used to think. *Once I ask her out, things will be simple.*

Well, that is, they would be simple . . . if the girl said yes. Fact of the matter is, I must not be attractive, because if I try to sit near them, they most certainly get up and walk away. They don't make it obvious or anything; almost as if they are just making a trip to the vending machines or to see another friend a few feet away. And then there are my feeble attempts at small talk. Whatever comes out of my mouth, something will come out of theirs that is calculated simply to end the conversation and shut me up so they can spy on the guys they actually do like. I have made up my mind that girls simply don't like me.

I've tried asking a girl out before, and boy did it go down in flames. It was a disaster beyond reasoning. You know, the sort of catastrophe you'd never see the likes of in a movie. It's always the same: Boy pines for beautiful, unattainable girl, hooks up with less-attractive girl next door at the end. Problem is, there's no girl next door for me. And since every other girl in my school qualifies as unattainable in comparison to the likes of me, Vegas oddsmakers will tell you I don't have a snowball's chance. And, you know, once a girl has made up her mind that she doesn't like you, that's it. Girls are a wonder to behold, but they are incredibly stubborn. The second she puts you in that "Out" box, forget all about her. Move on. She'll never set eyes on you again, so it's not worth your time to chase somebody who's already filed you away.

I don't know if I'll ever be in someone's "In" box. It might not happen until I meet new girls. Go to college. Enter the workforce. I can already tell she's out there somewhere, but she's certainly not here. The looks on these girls' faces when I walk around a corner or make eye contact don't exactly do wonders for my self-confidence. So I've given up on girls for now. They just don't seem to care. They will soon, though. Not these girls. Not at this place. Not now. Somewhere else I have yet to go. And that's one of the little things that makes life worth waiting for, you know? Thinking the journey's still in the future, still uncharted water, sort of helps me get through my day.

Oh, yes. This is supposed to be the part when I tell you that I've fallen in love with a great girl who really does like me, and I tell you never to give up. Nope. Hasn't happened yet. And I can safely assure you it never will at my high school. You might say, "Well, of course it won't with that attitude!" But an optimistic outlook wouldn't do any good, either. I used to be optimistic about it, but that got me nowhere.

However, there *is* a point to all this, and it goes something like this: She's out there. She's just not at your high school. So you're going to have to wait. Do some homework to occupy your time until then.

Brian Firenzi

For Better or For Worse®
by Lynn Johnston

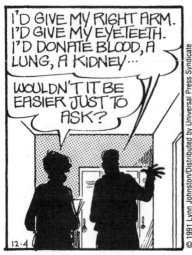

FOR BETTER OR FOR WORSE ©*United Features Syndicate. Reprinted by permission.*

The Single-for-Life Syndrome

The snow goose need not bathe to make itself white. Neither need you do anything but be yourself.

Lao-tzu

As my best friend so eloquently put it, we were "Rated PG," or platonically gifted. Always the shoulders for guys to cry on, we were the founders and co-presidents of the Never Been Kissed Club (in our area anyway; I'm sure there are other NBKCs out there), and were both still "proud" members at the ripe old age of nineteen. Both of us were intelligent, enthusiastic and active in clubs and sports. We had great senses of humor and were just as comfortable yelling at the refs from the stands as getting all primped to go out on the town.

Yet there existed a difference in our singleness. Melissa was single by choice. Granted, some of the guys who had pursued her were not exactly desirable, but the fact remains that they had pursued her. She had enjoyed a few minor almost-flings, but still claimed to be perpetually single. Now, when I say I hadn't ever had a boyfriend or even been pursued, this is not a "that-fling-with-the-guy-in-Ohio-last-summer-doesn't-count-because-we-won't-ever-see-each-other-again" statement. I didn't even have a kindergarten boyfriend. I had never been on a date, save for junior prom, which was an arranged thing—neither of us asked the other; someone just decided we should go together because our best friends were going together. It's not that I was antisocial or deathly afraid of boys; by the end of high school I hung out with about three times as many guys on a regular basis as girls. I was the eternal good friend whom any guy knew he could come to for advice on dating and how to snag the girl he wanted—it was just never me.

This was a source of longing, sadness, irritation, questioning and occasional misery for me. In most areas of my life I was quite stable, but for a few years every couple of months would yield a night of crying, generally catalyzed by a sappy movie or even just a song on the radio.

I came up with personal mottos such as, "If even the losers get lucky, then what does that make me?" and, "If nobody's going to be interested in you, you might as well be picky." While I constantly joked about my singleness, my insides were stinging. The sight of a happy couple on the street or in the mall would bring with it the knowledge that both of those people had found someone to hold, so why couldn't I? People I had graduated with were getting engaged, even married, but I couldn't get a date if my life depended on it. Testimonials from attached people who claimed to remember the deep despair I was experiencing did not make me feel better; rather they sent tidal waves crashing through the ocean of resentment building inside me.

After a few months at college, though, a funny thing happened. Even though my confidence in the relationship field did not improve, I began caring less and less.

My roommates, eerily similar to me in personality, were both in serious relationships, but instead of depressing me further, it helped me to think that maybe there was someone out there for me. My sophomore year I chose to live with the same two girls and another, also in a serious relationship, and everyone said it was *my* year—that Bec was gonna get some action on the dating scene. I wasn't so sure, but I didn't focus on it too much. College put enough on my mind without having to worry about being single for life. Besides, everyone told me love would find me when I wasn't looking for it.

So here I am, well into my sophomore year, *my* year, and here's where you're expecting me to start gushing about Mr. Right, the boyfriend I never thought I'd have—how he is the best thing that has ever happened to me and how I was silly to think I'd never get one because there really is someone out there for everyone. But no, this is not one of those "I got a significant other so you can, too!" musings that will just end up making someone more bitter. This is purely about a sorely needed attitude adjustment. I still have sporadic lonely nights, but I now know that I don't have to be alone to be lonely. I still love to torment my roommates and lay on the heavy guilt trips when they have date nights, or when I'm what I like to refer to as the "seventh wheel" on an outing with three couples and me, but this is mostly to see that look of amused frustration on their faces. I still make gagging noises when someone's being all lovey-dovey on the phone or talking about what her boyfriend did for her birthday. I still joke about being the first "gold plus" member of the NBKC. I still refuse to settle for less than what I want and deserve; perhaps I, too, am single by choice in that sense. I still haven't been kissed, but I'm okay with that. I live in hope.

Rebecca Ayres

Hoping to induce phone calls from potential dates,
Noreen performs an ancient tribal telephone dance.

Sweet-and-Sour Sixteen

If you can learn from hard knocks, you can also learn from soft touches.

Carolyn Kenmore

I was fifteen, soon to turn sixteen, and I felt pressured. I had never been kissed. I was certain I had to be one of the most backward, late-blooming teenagers there was, carrying around this terrible secret that might reveal itself at any moment—if I ever got a date.

My only consolation was that my best friend, Carol, was in the same predicament. She, too, feared the label "sweet sixteen and never been kissed."

We spent that summer plotting ways to absolve ourselves by meeting guys and getting dates. We even went so far as to sign ourselves up for corn detasseling. For three hot, sweaty weeks in humid Iowa, we walked up and down cornfields with a busload of teenagers, mostly guys, and picked corn. There were water fights, romps through the fields, heady compliments and serious flirtations—but no dates.

Carol had her sights set on one promising candidate (he

was at her side constantly), but when the last day of work came, he still had not asked her out. I think it was sheer frustration that drove her to tell him that she would be sixteen in two months and had never been kissed.

"You haven't?" he asked. "That's great! If you can go another two months without a kiss, you'll be sweet sixteen, not sour sixteen!"

So much for that candidate.

By the end of the summer, we had pretty much given up on our quest. We went out for pizza with a group of girls in another town. We were sitting there laughing and having a good time when two of the girls noticed a group of guys at a nearby table. Before long all the other girls had joined in and it was a full-on flirting party.

Carol and I became annoyed. Sure, the guys were cute. Sure, they were looking at us, but this was our last night of the summer! We weren't about to waste it on a group of guys who might send all kinds of positive signals then never make it to our table. We stomped outside to the parking lot to talk in peace. The guys followed us and asked if we knew the time.

They were even cuter close up. I tried not to stare at the one with dark, wavy hair and hazel eyes, but my eyes kept wandering back to him. His name was Cody.

The other girls soon joined us, and we talked with the guys as late as our curfews would allow. They arranged to meet us the next night at a park.

Somehow, the next night, we ended up paired off as couples. I found myself with Cody. He and I walked over to a monument in the park and sat down on it. Suddenly, anxiety overcame me. I realized that I was about to receive my first kiss, and I simply wasn't ready for it. I burst into tears. Cody put his arm around me and asked what was wrong. I blurted out the whole tragic story of being sixteen and having never been kissed. Then, realizing how lame this must have sounded, I went for broke. I blurted out every negative thing that had ever happened in my life. By the time I was done, I was convinced he must have thought I was a total nutcase.

He looked at me for a few moments from under those long, dark eyelashes, then slowly brushed his lips against mine. The kiss was soft, quick and moist. I was just glad when it was over—and that I was away from home. No one needed to know the embarrassment I had just put myself through. I never bothered to tell him how he could reach me again, and he never asked.

The next day, the phone rang and my mom answered. "It's for you," she said, a startled look in her eyes. As I walked over she whispered, "It's a boy!"

My heart went crazy. I managed to mumble a hello, and a male voice started talking. Cody! I felt as if my heart might burst out of my chest. Mom stared at me. I stared back. This was the first time that a boy who I cared about had called me.

I asked how he had gotten my number. He told me my girlfriend had given it to him and asked if I wanted to go out with him that weekend. He told me my girlfriend and his friend would be coming with us. "Would you like to go out with them?" he asked.

I'm not sure how I responded, but I know I accepted. I also said, "I never expected to hear from you again."

"Why not?" he asked.

"Well, after last night . . ."

"After last night, I think you're the sweetest girl I ever met," he said. There was a pause, then he added, "Someone has to sour you."

Ronica Stromberg

"I want our first date to be special.
Let's not spoil it by being ourselves."

First Kiss

It's a beautiful day, the summer before I start seventh grade. For Dee, it's the summer before eighth grade.

I'm watching TV. *Jenny Jones* is on. The guests argue about their unfaithful husbands or wives, while their wives or husbands deny all of the accusations of infidelity. Suddenly, Dee plops down next to me on the couch, coming from the bathroom. She nuzzles very close to me and rests her head on my shoulder, complaining about how bony it is. I tell her to shut up. I feel very conscious of her head on my shoulder, and then I feel conscious of her staring at me. I look at her and smile.

"What's up?" I ask, confused.

"Nothing," she answers, shaking her head.

She nuzzles even closer to me, and I feel awkward. Her arm slides in between my arm and my body, and she clings to me. A billion thoughts race through my head and then all of a sudden . . . nothing. I feel her staring at me, the heat of her face close to mine. I look at her, and I see three eyes. She looks straight into my eyes, pinning me with her gaze, locking my eyes with hers.

"Don't you wanna kiss me?" she asks sweetly.

My mouth drops open, and I quickly close it, realizing

that it was not the right look to give. I start to sweat a little. What's worse, I feel her arms snake around my neck. I glance down for a second, sensing an awkwardness, like she doesn't know what she's doing. I look up again into her big green eyes. Her confidence suddenly blows me away, and I am intimidated. Time ceases to pass in minutes or even seconds . . . but in milliseconds. Actually, the only time that exists is measured by the small movements that she makes.

A smile slowly forms on her lips.

I start to blush, feeling my blood rush into my cheeks, and I feel stupid, like I don't know what I'm doing, which I don't. And in that moment I curse her for making me feel stupid; she knows what she's doing to me.

I have to do something. Her next move might be an embarrassing question, like, "Do you not know how to kiss or something?" or "Are you a prude?" or "What's wrong with you, boy?" She's too close to me. She's moving too fast for me. She's too close to my face! She's too intimidating. She's too . . . cute!

She stops smiling.

Oh no! What's she thinking now? I'm so stupid! I should've done something! She thinks I'm a prude! I am! So what?!?!? So, I'm a prude. Give me a break! Give . . . me . . . a break!

She wets her lips.

Whoa.

Her face inches closer.

Oh, man. Only a breath away from my face now, I see her lips form a smile before she presses hers to mine.

Slow, soft and sweet. Only her arms around me keep me from flying.

After what seems like a few minutes, she stops kissing me and looks up. Her emerald eyes sparkle, and she smiles. She giggles and says that I'm cute. I stare at her. She nuzzles back against me and watches TV. I sit there, staring at her, dumbfounded . . . with a stupid smile pasted on my lips.

Wow.

Ron Cheng

Changes and the Game "High School"

School is a battlefield for your heart.

Angela, My So-Called Life

In the still darkness of my bedroom, my mind wandered unrestrained by the four walls that created boundaries for my body. I could not see a single thing. My vision was blurred without my glasses, leaving only my mind to see things in focus.

For the past year my life had been spinning out of control. I was becoming disoriented in a world I had once seen with vision as clear as crystal. Everything was changing. My friends were being lost to boyfriends, crushes and obsessions. The world that revolved around me was being dismantled, smashed and demolished by the people who had helped make it. Everything was falling apart, and I couldn't stop it.

Things were changing. "High school is a place to grow, to experiment and to change," someone once told a scared, unsure eighth-grader on the fateful first day at a whole new game with rules unknown. I didn't want to ever change, and so I tried to make a square block fit into a circular hole. Needless to say, it did not work. I spent a whole year in lies—black destructive lies that I now regret and would rather forget. I tried to follow my friends in all that they did, positive that they knew better. At parties, I tried what everyone else did, but the next day I realized I had not had that much fun.

My friends were trying to help me fit into this mold, and it hurt to be prodded, poked and squeezed like a tube of toothpaste just to try to fit in. All of the things I had promised myself before entering high school just didn't seem to apply. I grew silly, obnoxious, like a crybaby or a little girl. I did not mature; I grew immature. I thought I was cute and likable. What I did not realize was that I was a fraud. I tried to be like everyone else. I started to dress in the same clone-like fashions, talk, write and even eat the same way.

Later that year a new girl arrived in high school. I decided to support her by being a life raft for a while. Little did I expect that she would start to copy me. Like everyone else, I pretended to know what I was doing. As she spent more and more time with me, I realized that little things like her choice of words, hand gestures and her attitude were all annoying. One gray, gloomy day, I had taped myself giving a speech and when I played it back, it did not sound like me. I could not recognize the voice on the tape for a while and then it hit me. The attitude and persona portrayed through my voice was like hers. I was the same. From that moment I detested myself. Through this hatred, a window opened and for a nanosecond I saw the girl who didn't care what everyone else thought, who always stood up for others and who had friends who loved her just the way she was. She was the real me. Full of determination, I started the long, perilous hike back to individuality. On the way up, I found pieces of myself that I had lost along the way. My life had become a long quest in which I was to search for priceless capsules holding my identity and to put them back in the treasury of my soul. The quest is undoubtedly not over, but I gain more freedom every day. I now surprise my friends and myself with values and morals I didn't know I possessed and I no longer just take others' words for truth anymore.

I realized high school is a game we all play. We are thrown into a big pool with no one yelling expectations, instructions or the objective. We are forced to sink or swim. Perhaps I have seen the light, the truth and the goal of high school. Or perhaps I have only opened my eyes to a bigger stage of shadows and illusions. Who really knows?

Adelene Wong

A Toast

Raise your glass to the sky
with hopes and dreams held high.
To the graduates I toast . . .

Here's to the friends we've lost and gained,
and the people we'll never know by name.
To the bonds that we've made and albums we filled,
memories that may fade but never be killed.

Here's to the phone calls filled with tears,
and to the hours spent talking away our fears.
To the people we thought deserved our hearts,
whom now we bash and rip apart.

Here's to the pictures in frames with stories to say,
that we will be sure to pack when we go away.
To the football games we have watched beneath the lights,
and our cheers and chants drifting into the night.

Here's to proms and dances,
and high-school romances.
To homecoming games,
with all the wins in our name.

Here's to late nights we've spent cramming for tests,
and mornings where coffee made up for our rest.
To the dances and events we took months to create,
the night before worries that came too late.

Here's to the tears we knew we'd cry,
to the people and places we say good-bye.
To the wild and bizarre things we've done,
that we will remember to be the most fun.

Here's to the letters we left unsigned,
may our identities be revealed all in due time.
To the relationships we wonder how we ever lived without,
and the crushes we look back on and laugh about.

So now it is time to place our glasses down,
put our caps on and turn our tassels around.
Listen for our names and let them echo through,
and realize how fast these four years just flew.

Sarah Watroba

More Chicken Soup?

Many of the stories and poems that you have read in this book were submitted by readers like you who have read *Chicken Soup for the Teenage Soul* and other *Chicken Soup for the Soul* books. We would love to have you contribute a story, poem or letter to a future *Chicken Soup for the Teenage Soul* book. This may be a story you write yourself, or one you clip out of your school newspaper, local newspaper, church bulletin or a magazine. It might be something you read in a book or found on the Internet. It could also be a favorite poem, quotation or cartoon you have saved. Please send as much information as you know about where it came from.

You may send a copy of your stories or other pieces to us at this address:

Chicken Soup for the Teenage Soul
P.O. Box 936
Pacific Palisades, CA 90272
e-mail: *stories@iam4teens.com*
Web site: *www.iam4teens.com*

Supporting Teenagers

With each *Chicken Soup for the Teenage Soul* book that we publish, we designate one or more charities that are doing important work for teens to receive a portion of the profits that are generated. We are making a donation to the following charity:

Soup and Support for Teachers and Teens

Soup and Support for Teachers and Teens gives teachers the opportunity to use the *Chicken Soup for the Teenage Soul* books free of charge along with a guidebook called *101 Ways to Use Chicken Soup in the Classroom*. If you would like to know more about this program and find out ways you can help or be a recipient of this program, contact:

Soup and Support for Teachers and Teens
P.O. Box 999
Pacific Palisades, CA 90272
phone: 310-573-3655
e-mail: *soupandsupport@iam4teens.com*

Who Is Jack Canfield?

Jack Canfield is a bestselling author and one of America's leading experts in the development of human potential. He is both a dynamic and entertaining speaker and a highly sought-after trainer with a wonderful ability to inform and inspire audiences to open their hearts, love more openly and boldly pursue their dreams.

Jack spent his teenage years growing up in Martins Ferry, Ohio, and Wheeling, West Virginia, with his sister Kimberly (Kirberger) and his two brothers, Rick and Taylor. The whole family has spent most of their professional careers dedicated to educating, counseling and empowering teens. Jack admits to being shy and lacking self-confidence in high school, but through a lot of hard work he earned letters in three sports and graduated third in his class.

After graduating college, Jack taught high school in the inner city of Chicago and in Iowa. In recent years, Jack has expanded this to include adults in both educational and corporate settings.

He is the author and narrator of several bestselling audio- and videocassette programs. He is a regularly consulted expert for radio and television broadcasts and has published numerous books—all bestsellers within their categories—including more than thirty *Chicken Soup for the Soul* books, *The Aladdin Factor, Heart at Work, 100 Ways to Build Self-Concept in the Classroom* and *Dare to Win.*

Jack addresses over one hundred groups each year. His clients include professional associations, school districts, government agencies, churches and corporations in all fifty states.

Jack conducts an annual eight-day Training of Trainers program in the areas of building self-esteem and achieving peak performance. It attracts educators, counselors, parenting trainers, corporate trainers, professional speakers, ministers and others interested in developing their speaking and seminar-leading skills in these areas.

For further information about Jack's books, tapes and trainings, or to schedule him for a presentation, please contact:

The Canfield Training Group
P.O. Box 30880 • Santa Barbara, CA 93130
phone: 800-237-8336 • fax: 805-563-2945
e-mail: *speaking@canfieldgroup.com*
Web site: *www.chickensoup.com*

Who Is Mark Victor Hansen?

Mark Victor Hansen is a professional speaker who, in the last twenty years, has made over four thousand presentations to more than two million people in thirty-three countries. His presentations cover sales excellence and strategies; personal empowerment and development; and how to triple your income and double your time off.

Mark has spent a lifetime dedicated to his mission of making a profound and positive difference in people's lives. Throughout his career, he has inspired hundreds of thousands of people to create a more powerful and purposeful future for themselves while stimulating the sale of billions of dollars worth of goods and services.

Mark is a prolific writer and has authored *Future Diary, How to Achieve Total Prosperity* and *The Miracle of Tithing.* He is the coauthor of the *Chicken Soup for the Soul* series, *Dare to Win* and *The Aladdin Factor* (all with Jack Canfield) and *The Master Motivator* (with Joe Batten).

Mark has also produced a complete library of personal empowerment audio- and videocassette programs that have enabled his listeners to recognize and better use their innate abilities in their business and personal lives. His message has made him a popular television and radio personality with appearances on ABC, NBC, CBS, HBO, PBS, QVC and CNN.

He has also appeared on the cover of numerous magazines, including *Success, Entrepreneur* and *Changes.*

Mark is a big man with a heart and a spirit to match—an inspiration to all who seek to better themselves.

For further information about Mark, please contact:

Mark Victor Hansen & Associates
P.O. Box 7665
Newport Beach, CA 92658
phone: 949-759-9304 or 800-433-2314
fax: 949-722-6912
Web site: *www.chickensoup.com*

Who Is Kimberly Kirberger?

Kimberly is an advocate for teens, a writer for teens, a mother of a teen, and a friend and confidante to the many teens in her life. She is committed to bettering the lives of teens around the globe through her books and the outreach she does for teens on behalf of her organization, Inspiration and Motivation for Teens, Inc.

Kim's love for teens was first expressed globally with the publication of the bestselling *Chicken Soup for the Teenage Soul*. This book was a true labor of love for Kim, and the result of years of friendship and research with teens from whom she learned what really matters. After the success of the first *Teenage Soul* book, and the outpouring of hundreds and thousands of letters and submissions from teens around the world, Kim went on to coauthor the *New York Times* #1 bestsellers *Chicken Soup for the Teenage Soul II* and *Chicken Soup for the Teenage Soul III*, *Chicken Soup for the Teenage Soul Journal*, *Chicken Soup for the Teenage Soul Letters*, *Chicken Soup for the Teenage Soul on Tough Stuff* and *Chicken Soup for the College Soul*. Kim's empathic understanding of the issues affecting parents led her to coauthor *Chicken Soup for the Parent's Soul*.

In October 1999, the first book in Kim's *Teen Love* series was released. *Teen Love: On Relationships* has since become a *New York Times* bestseller. Her friendship and collaboration with Colin Mortensen of MTV's *Real World Hawaii* produced the much-loved *Teen Love: A Journal on Relationships* and *Teen Love: On Friendship*. She recently released *Teen Love: A Journal on Friendship*.

Her nonprofit organization, Soup and Support for Teachers, is committed to providing inspirational and supportive reading materials to teens and teachers.

When she is not reading letters she gets from teens, Kim is offering them support and encouragement in the forums on her Web site, *www.iam4teens.com*. She also enjoys nurturing her family, listening to her son's band and hanging out with her friends.

For information or to schedule Kim for a presentation, contact:

I.A.M. 4 Teens, Inc.
P.O. Box 936
Pacific Palisades, CA 90272
e-mail for stories: *stories@iam4teens.com*
e-mail for letters and feedback: *kim@iam4teens.com*
Web site: *www.iam4teens.com*

Contributors

Some of the stories in this book were taken from previously published sources, such as books and magazines. These sources are acknowledged in the permissions section.

Most of the stories were contributed by readers of our previous *Chicken Soup for the Soul* books who responded to our requests for stories. If you would like to contact them, you can reach them at their e-mail addresses provided below.

Sami Armin is a biology student at the University of Western Ontario in London, Ontario, Canada. She enjoys playing tennis, golf and writing poetry, and hopes to someday publish a series of poetry books. Her poem is dedicated to her parents and aunts. She can be reached at *gidget1358@hotmail.com.*

Rebecca Ayres received a psychology degree from Santa Clara University and currently volunteers full-time. She plans on earning a master's in social work to become a counselor. Her story is dedicated to her wonderfully supportive friends, her ex-roommates and their significant others, her family and NBKC members everywhere (especially Melissa). She can be reached by e-mail at *RebeccaLA@yahoo.com.*

James D. Barron is the author of *She's Having a Baby—And I'm Having a Breakdown, She's Had a Baby—And I'm Having a Meltdown,* and *She Wants a Ring—And I Don't Wanna Change a Thing.* He can be reached at *jdbarron6@aol.com.*

Jennifer Baxton is a writer currently living in a "weird" suburb of Los Angeles. An alumni of AmeriCorps, she has been trained as a red-carded firefighter and a national park ranger. Currently, Jennifer teaches writing compositions at too many community colleges in Southern California. She can be reached at *goobiesun@yahoo.com.*

Marjee Berry-Wellman is a Christian author and proud mother of Jeff, Josh and Julie, as well as her angel baby, Melanie. Writing is Marjee's passion, and she hopes to leave readers with something solid to digest. Born and raised in Sterling, Illinois, Marjee currently resides in Clarion, Iowa. She welcomes feedback at *mrjwell@goldfieldaccess.net.*

Amanda Bertrand attends Cook College at Rutgers University in New Jersey. This is her first published work, and she is extremely excited. She would like to thank her family and friends for always being there for her. She dedicates this work to Ken R. Brams. She can be reached at *RutgersAngel@aol.com.*

Hannah Brandys is twenty-two years old and lives in Toronto, Canada. She wrote "The First" when she was fifteen, and she is thrilled to have the chance to share it with others. Hannah's hobbies include reading, writing, skiing, kickboxing and traveling. She can be reached at *hannahbran@yahoo.com.*

Noah Campana is an English and psychology major who gives talks to teens about sex and relationships. He enjoys running, climbing and sleeping. He knows karate and seventeen other Japanese words and is best known for spontaneously singing, "Play that Funky Music White Boy." This and everything else he does is dedicated to God— "you rock!" He can be reached at *lord-biohazarrd@hotmail.com.*

Amy Catalano is a college student who enjoys writing creatively in her free time. This is her first attempt at publication, and she'd like to pursue a career in writing later in life. She can be reached at *amybabe126@yahoo.com*.

Linda Chiara is a freelance writer in Connecticut. Her work has appeared in *Reader's Digest, Ladies' Home Journal, Boys' Life, The Christian Science Monitor, Family Circle* and *Baby Talk*. She also writes regularly for parenting magazines. She is married and has three terrific sons. She can be reached at *chiarapub@hotmail.com*.

Adam Cohen lives in Maui, Hawaii. He is currently working in the health-food industry. He is an accomplished pianist of eleven years and has played in many presentations. He is an inspiring writer and poet. This story is dedicated to his best friend and truest brother, David Byrne.

Melissa Collette is a twenty-one-year-old college student living in California. Some of her other works can be found in *Chicken Soup for the Teenage Soul II* and *Teen Love: On Friendship*. She is grateful for the opportunity to inspire teens through her poetry. She can be reached at *yourmkangel@yahoo.com*.

Cheryl Costello-Forshey's poetry has been published in numerous *Chicken Soup* books as well as *Stories for a Teen's Heart, Stories for a Faithful Heart, Stories for a Teen's Heart 2* and *A Pleasant Place*. She can be reached at *costello-forshey@1st.net*.

Amanda Cuda is a full-time reporter for the *Connecticut Post* newspaper, based in Bridgeport, Connecticut. She is also a freelance writer whose work has appeared in *Language* magazine, *FamilyClick.com* and the Great Lakes Radio Consortium. She can be reached at *cudaaman@yahoo.com*.

Molly Day wrote her poem at the age of thirteen. She is now sixteen years old and a junior at Carmel High School where she is involved in student government, National Honor Society and varsity soccer. She hopes to study premed in college, while simultaneously pursuing a major in English. She can be reached at *SunEday8@aol.com*.

Scott Diel lives in Fayetteville, Arkansas. He can be reached at *sdiel@uark.edu*.

Delicia Dudley is now a college freshman in the Tri-Cities of Washington. She dedicates this story to anyone who has ever made a mistake.

Ashleigh Dumas is a student at the University of Western Ontario in London, Ontario, Canada. In her spare time she enjoys skiing, writing and hanging out with friends and family. She would like to dedicate her story to her grandfather, Michael Nelligan, and is happy to announce that his prediction for her when she was a little girl has come true: She has found her true love—her high-school sweetheart, Luke.

Jonathan Evans is from Tunkhannock, Pennsylvania, and is now an English and human development double-major at Boston College. His piece, written in high school, is dedicated to all of those he loves—his teachers, friends and especially his father, mother and sister. He can be reached at *jonathan.evans.3@bc.edu*.

Melinda Favreau is a junior at Mt. Ararat High School, where she plays field hockey and the flute. She is a staff member of her community's teen newspaper, as well as her school's newspaper. She was the winner of *Teen* magazine's 1998 reader fiction contest. She can be reached at *kawaiitokyorose@hotmail.com*.

Anne G. Fegely, nineteen years old, currently attends James Madison University in pursuit of an English degree and secondary education minor. Her hobbies include writing poetry, sketching portraits and powerlifting. Her poetry has been published in the *Teen Love* series. She would like to dedicate her poem to her parents and Mrs. Getz.

Brian Firenzi is a sophomore in high school in California. He enjoys creating videos with his friends, writing screenplays and snowboarding. Brain aspires to work in journalism or filmmaking. He can be reached at *bfirenzi@earthlink.net.*

Molly Gaebler is a fifteen-year-old high-school student in Berkeley, California. She enjoys writing and is a reporter for her school newspaper, the Berkeley High Jacket. In addition to writing, she takes pleasure in dancing, playing goalie for her field hockey team and playing lacrosse. She can be reached at *Starlette8646@aol.com.*

Erin Gandia is sixteen years old and a junior at Carthage Central High School. An honor-roll student, Erin is involved in theater and enjoys listening to and performing music. Her parents and friends are very important aspects in her life. She can be reached at *sweetangel14259@yahoo.com.*

Gwynne Garfinkle lives in Los Angeles. Her poetry, fiction, essays and music reviews have appeared in numerous publications, including *Chicken Soup for the Teenage Soul on Tough Stuff, Exquisite Corpse, Big Bridge, The American Voice, Loca* and the Los Angeles *New Times.*

Ambrosia Gilchrist is a freelance writer in Saskatoon, Saskatchewan, Canada. In her short writing career, she has been published numerous times for her poetry, and has had artworks placed in galleries in her hometown. She loves sports and all of the arts. She is currently in the ninth grade in the advanced program at Bedford Road Collegiate.

Randy Glasbergen is one of America's most widely and frequently published cartoonists. More than 25,000 of his cartoons have been published by *Funny Times, Good Housekeeping, Cosmopolitan, Guideposts for Teens, Campus Life,* America Online and many others. His daily comic panel "The Better Half" is syndicated worldwide by King Features Syndicate. He is also the author of three cartooning instruction books and several cartoon anthologies. You can find more of Randy's cartoons online at *www.glasbergen.com.*

Kristy Glassen is a student at Penn State University. As a senior graduating in December, she wanted to take this opportunity to say thank-you to those people who have stuck by her side through it all. They know who they are. To her family, Mom, Dad and Ryan, she thanks them for believing in her and giving her the courage to chase her dreams. Her love goes out to them. This quote sums up how she looks at life, "I am not afraid of tomorrow. I have seen yesterday, and I love today." She can be reached at *psukristy21@hotmail.com.*

Benedicta Goveia is a ninth-grade student living in Toronto, Canada. She enjoys reading and writing to a great extent and is aspiring to get her first book published by her sixteenth birthday. Her other interests include collecting Harry Potter items and playing the piano.

Nicole Hamberger is a sixteen-year-old optimist who loves to give back to her community. Aside from her passion for writing, she volunteers at Saint Barnabas Hospital twice a week, working in both the emergency room and the Child Care Development Center. She also teaches religious education and enjoys spending time with her friends.

Amy Hilborn is an honors English student at Redeemer University College in Ancaster, Ontario, hoping to pursue a master's degree in creative writing. She has been published at her university and the Poetry Institute of Canada. Written when seventeen years old, this story is dedicated to her family and her boyfriend, Colin.

Jayme Johnson is a college student. This is her first published piece. She would like to thank her friends and family for supporting her, Chrissie for being her best friend for ten years and running, and her boyfriend, Chris, for always being there for her. She can be reached at *sportysweetie10@cs.com.*

Bret Anthony Johnston is a writer in northern Michigan. This story is dedicated to his brother, Bill.

Caitlin Keryc is a student at Columbia University. Though she has not decided on a major, she's living it up in New York City and enjoying all that college life has to offer. She wrote this story for her junior year writing class in high school. She can be reached at *cbk2001@columbia.edu.*

Cassie Kirby lives in Livonia, Michigan. She is currently in college, studying to be an elementary-school teacher. She would like to thank her family, her boyfriend and her best friends for their unwavering support and constant laughs. She can be reached at *KirbAngel@aol.com.*

Sarah Klapak is a high-school student living in Wyoming, Ontario, Canada. She coaches recreational gymnastics, enjoys writing short stories and poems, has aspirations of becoming a teacher of the deaf and is strong in her Christian faith. She can be reached at *saray_bo_barah11@hotmail.com.*

Michelle LaNoce is a college student in New York. She is a very outgoing person who lives life to the fullest, always seeking out new opportunities and striving to obtain her many goals. She can be reached at *sunshineml@juno.com.*

Paula Leifer is currently a dance and English education major at the University of Maryland. This story was written when she was a sophomore in high school, and she hopes to continue pursuing her writing career throughout college. She can be reached at *niketah@wam.umd.edu.*

Kathryn Litzenberger is a student at the University of Rhode Island where she is majoring in secondary education and English. She has been previously published in *Chicken Soup for the Teenage Soul.* This piece is dedicated to her best friend, Erin, who has never let her down. She can be reached at *Klit1352@postoffice.uri.edu.*

Laura Loken is currently a freshman majoring in elementary education at the University of North Dakota. She is a past contributor to *Chicken Soup for the Teenage Soul III* and is excited about being part of the series again. She can be reached at *laurabeth_27@ hotmail.com.*

Joanna Long wrote her piece when was fifteen years old. She still enjoys writing, but her favorite study is history. She likes to play soccer, swim, take part in almost any outdoor activity and hang out with her friends. She can be reached at *JoBoo1013@aol.com.*

Eleanor Luken is an amateur high-school writer from Louisville, Kentucky. She can be reached at *ellieluken@aol.com.*

Anna Maier is a first-year college student in Michigan. She is working toward a degree in education with hopes of teaching the hearing-impaired. She submitted her piece as part of a final exam in her high-school English class. Anna can be reached at *Brainsync2@aol.com.*

Cortney Martin has been writing since age ten and penned "What I Really Learned in World Geography" as a high-school senior. Now a college sophomore, Cortney is on staff at *The Pasadena Citizen* newspaper and writes short stories in her spare time. She can be reached at *ozindiscoworld@juno.com.*

Paige Melillo is a 2002 graduate of Boston University's College of Communications. She can be reached at *Dreamer17p@aol.com.*

Dan Mulhausen just graduated from Columbia Basin Community College. He is now attending school at the University of Oregon. Since the story was written, Dan and Tash have unfortunately gone separate ways, but they remain close friends. He can be reached at *Rudy63@aol.com.*

Laura O'Neill is a freelance writer in Ellicott City, Missouri. She is sixteen years old and attends Mount de Sales Academy. She is very involved in her parish's youth ministry program and hopes to pursue a career as a youth minister. Laura can be reached at *squeakylaughter@hotmail.com.*

Lorelei Pablo is a twenty-one-year-old immigrant from the Philippines. She arrived in the United States on November 30, 2001. She is working full-time as a certified nursing assistant in one of the best nursing homes in her home state. She enjoys writing poems in her leisure time. She also has plans to continue her studies in the near future.

Michael T. Powers, whose writing appears in many inspirational teen books, is a high-school girls' coach, youth director and the author of his own book, *Straight from the Heart.* For a sneak peek or to join the thousands of worldwide readers on his daily inspirational e-mail list, visit *www.HeartTouchers.com.* He can also be reached at *MichaelTPowers@aol.com.*

Sara Profitt will graduate with the Class of 2003 at Brookville High School in Ohio. She is involved in several clubs and has been a staff member of her school newspaper every year of high school. Sara plans to attend college where she will major in English and theater. This poem is dedicated to Chris. She can be reached at *SaraBell224@aol.com.*

Zihanna Rahman is seventeen years old and wrote "Sorrows Underneath" in her sophomore year of high school. She started writing stories in elementary school, but moved on to poetry and lyrics in high school. She finds inspiration through music and art. Her other writings can be found on her Web site at *neverlast.cjb.net.* She can be reached at *yb_zihan@hotmail.com.*

Jennifer Reichert is a freelance writer in Los Angeles, where she is currently an undergraduate at UCLA, majoring in English. She recently studied at Cambridge University, England. She is also a former staff member for the UCLA *Daily Bruin,* and presently interns for a film production company.

Marissa Roche will be completing her junior year in high school this spring. She attends Gardner High School in Gardner, Massachusetts. She is very active in her school and her community. She loves to write poetry and has been published in anthologies from *Poetry.com.* She can be reached at *mlroche@juno.com.*

Katherine Rowe is a student in college and plans to major in English. She enjoys writing and attending acting workshops. She is a loyal reader of the entire Chicken Soup series and became inspired by the books to write her own story. Katherine can be reached at *Punkey00@hotmail.com.*

Jodi Rudin is a high-school senior. She enjoys reading and writing short stories. She facilitates The Pacific Institute's curriculum *Increasing Your Causative Power,* which is a self-help program for teens. This story is in memory of Mary Scharlach. She can be reached at *rudi_07@hotmail.com.*

Amanda Russell is a resident of Tennessee, who enjoys writing poems and short stories. She is pursuing a Bachelor of Science degree in theater education at Middle Tennessee State University. This story is dedicated to her best friend, Kristen Hrusovsky. She can be reached at *meow_kitten@hotmail.com.*

Michelle Siil is a girl of many words. "Breathing" is her first published work, hopefully one of many. When Michelle graduates from college in 2006, she hopes to become a teacher and a writer. She appreciates the support of her family, friends and teachers. Michelle can be reached at *Rosesx10k@hotmail.com*.

Rebecca Slobada is a student at Translyvania University in Lexington, Kentucky. She is studying art and psychology and will graduate in 2005. She can be reached at *Beckabeth01@aol.com*.

Bobbi Smith is partner in a Baha'i-inspired socioeconomic development project based on Vancouver Island, British Columbia. Her story is dedicated to Norman and Toni Smith, Erika Hastings Adlparvar, the Smiths, the Sabripours and all those who have enabled her to serve. She can be reached at *ilikebikes1234@yahoo.com*.

Ronica Stromberg has written for many publications and is the author of the young adult mystery, *The Glass Inheritance* published by Royal Fireworks Press. She is currently at work on a teen series to be published by Moody Press. She can be reached at *ronicak@yahoo.com*.

Jenifer Sunday is a high-school student in Massachusetts. She plans to attend college in the fall and will major in art education. Her poetry has also been published in *Devotions of the Mind*. This poem is dedicated to her dearest friends. She can be reached at *Akaswish@aol.com*.

Allison Thorp is a freshman at West Virginia Wesleyan College majoring in music education and English. She enjoys playing the piano, especially for the college jazz ensemble. She is secretary for her class and is active in Kappa Phi, a Christian woman's organization. She can be reached at *a_thorp@wvwc.edu*.

Pegah Vaghaye started writing poetry and short stories as early as eight years old. Since then, she has been a member of several writing organizations and has contributed her works to youth and church newsletters and magazines. She hopes to publish her compilation of poems someday. She may be reached at *pegah_vaghaye@hotmail.com*.

Christy Vander Griendt is educating herself toward a career in forensics and pathology at Camosun College in Victoria, British Columbia, Canada. Her passion for poetry is what led her to write the poem, "One Step Behind," which was written for and dedicated to her sister.

Christine Walsh is a comedian and actress in Boston, Massachusetts. Outside of the spotlight, she is a nanny for two beautiful and adventurous toddlers, Jacob and Joshua. Christine wishes to thank David for his love and ability to always make her smile.

Staci Warren wrote this poem when she was twelve years old during a hard time for her family. Her stepdad had just died and she wanted to cheer up her mother. She is fourteen years old and goes to Allen High School. She is glad she has made it this far and believes in "never stop dreaming."

Sarah Watroba is a freshman at Oswego State University. She is majoring in broadcasting and plans to pursue a career in the television or radio industry. Her poem is dedicated to the class of 2001 of North Tonawanda High School. It was read to all of the graduates on their final day in high school at an assembly dedicated to taking the next step in life. The class of 2001 was her inspiration for writing this poem. She will never forget the memories they shared and the lessons that she learned during those unforgettable four years. Best of luck to all future graduates. She can be reached at *Sarah5416@aol.com*.

Jennifer Winkelman works in the marketing research industry. Her understanding and hardworking husband truly proves that finding the man of your dreams is possible!

This story is dedicated to her best friend, "Mary Anne," who was there for her through everything. Jenny can be reached at *mdtwnqt1@aol.com*.

Adelene Wong is currently a senior in the International Baccalaureate program. She wants to thank her mother and sister for all the support they've given over the years. She wishes to share this thought: *A closed mind is a good thing to lose. Be open, honest and empathetic. You will get a lot further than you think!*

Rebecca Woolf is a freelance writer and photographer who has written for *Chicken Soup for the Teenage Soul II* and *III, Teen Love: On Relationships, Teen Love: On Friendship, Teen Love: A Journal on Friendship, 19* (the popular UK magazine) and more. Keep your eyes out for Rebecca's first solo book of poetry titled, *Through Broken Mirrors: A Reflective Memoir.* Rebecca is the program director and newsletter editor for Lead the Star, a creative company devoted to inspiring creativity and strength of identity in young adults. She can be reached at *rebeccawoolf@hotmail.com*.

Pey Jung Yeong is a seventeen-year-old college student currently studying in Australia. Born in Malaysia, she was actively involved in debates and essay competitions in her high-school days. She enjoys reading, writing and playing the piano in her spare time. She can be reached at *ypjung@hotmail.com*.

Kelley Youmans is a junior at Michigan State majoring in English education. This is her first publication, but she has been on *YM's* news team and writes daily. She dedicates this story to her family and friends for their support and to her sister Sarah. She can be reached at *KellJuneBug@hotmail.com*.

Permissions *(continued from page iv)*

Lucky. Reprinted by permission of Ambrosia Gilchrist. ©2001 Ambrosia Gilchrist.

Two of Me. Reprinted by permission of Anne G. Fegely. ©2000 Anne G. Fegely.

What I Really Learned in World Geography. Reprinted by permission of Cortney Martin. ©2000 Cortney Martin.

I Finally Did It. Reprinted by permission of Katherine Rowe. ©1999 Katherine Rowe.

And There He Was. Reprinted by permission of Joanna Long. ©2000 Joanna Long.

My Secret in Silence. Reprinted by permission of Lorelei Pablo. ©1999 Lorelei Pablo.

Reflections. Reprinted by permission of Paige Melillo. ©1999 Paige Melillo.

The Sound of Silence. Reprinted by permission of Rebecca Woolf. ©2000 Rebecca Woolf.

In Love. Reprinted by permission of Michelle LaNoce. ©2000 Michelle LaNoce.

Breathing. Reprinted by permission Michelle Siil. ©2001 Michelle Siil.

My Best Friend. Reprinted by permission of Jayme Johnson. ©2000 Jayme Johnson.

Teenage Love. Reprinted by permission of Molly Day. ©1998 Molly Day.

Always. Reprinted by permission of Amy Catalano. ©2001 Amy Catalano.

Living Without You. Reprinted by permission of Kristy Glassen. ©2000 Kristy Glassen.

Late-Night Talk. Reprinted by permission of Nicole Hamberger. ©2001 Nicole Hamberger.

The First. Reprinted by permission of Hannah Brandys. ©1999 Hannah Brandys.

One of Those Days. Reprinted by permission of Cassie Kirby. ©2000 Cassie Kirby.

Sand Castles. Reprinted by permission of Jennifer Reichert. ©1998 Jennifer Reichert.

When We Risk It All. Reprinted by permission of Kristy Glassen. ©2001 Kristy Glassen.

Tinfoil and a Hair Ribbon. Reprinted by permission of Cheryl Costello-Forshey. ©2002 Cheryl Costello-Forshey.

Saying Good-Bye. Reprinted by permission of Kathryn Litzenberger. ©2000 Kathryn Litzenberger.

I Hope. Reprinted by permission of Laura O'Neill. ©2000 Laura O'Neill.

Losing My Best Friend. Reprinted by permission of Amanda Russell. ©1999 Amanda Russell.

My Friend Andrea. Reprinted by permission of Laura Loken. ©2000 Laura Loken.